S0-ARW-982

Under
the
Shadow

Also by Anne Knowles
The Halcyon Island

Under
the
Shadow

by Anne Knowles

1 8 1 7

HARPER & ROW, PUBLISHERS

Cambridge, Philadelphia, San Francisco, London, Mexico City, São Paulo, Sydney

NEW YORK

The publisher wishes to thank John Betjeman and John Murray (Publishers) Ltd., for their kind permission to quote lines from *Hunter Trials* taken from the *Collected Poems*.

Under the Shadow
Copyright © 1983 by Anne Knowles
All rights reserved. No part of this book may be used or reproduced in any manner whatsoever without written permission except in the case of brief quotations embodied in critical articles and reviews. Printed in the United States of America. For information address Harper & Row, Publishers, Inc., 10 East 53rd Street, New York, N.Y. 10022.
First American Edition

Library of Congress Cataloging in Publication Data
Knowles, Anne.
  Under the shadow.

  Summary: Fifteen-year-old Cathy helps her friend
Mark, who has muscular dystrophy, find a sense of
freedom when she gets a horse for him to ride.
  [1. Muscular dystrophy—Fiction. 2. Physically
handicapped—Fiction. 3. Horses—Fiction. 4. Friendship—Fiction] I. Title.
PZ7.K7618Un 1983   [Fic]   82-48857
ISBN 0-06-023221-8
ISBN 0-06-023222-6 (lib. bdg.)

1 2 3 4 5 6 7 8 9 10

Under
the
Shadow

One

There would be an hour yet before it was dark. Cathy went out into the garden, under the bare, angled branches of the trees, and wondered what the place would be like when summer came. Behind her the white walls of the old house gleamed pale against the shadows of the forest. She shivered, with the coolness of the air, with excitement, with a suspicion of apprehension. This was a good place, and she was glad they had come, but she had not rid herself of all her doubts. It had been such a sudden change, such a quick uprooting. It hardly seemed a moment since Dad had opened that letter, saying he had been left a house by his great-uncle John: an old house with five acres of land in the forest. "Beamsters," it was called: and they had driven down to inspect it and found an ancient, timbered, haphazard sort of house set down in the forest as if in the palm of a great green hand.

Dad had walked in the garden and turned the rich soil with his boot; he had walked through the house and felt the solid strength of it. Inside, each of its rooms seemed on a different level from any other: there were steps up, and slopes down, and everywhere the timbers showed themselves as freely as they might in a ship. From the end corners of the house, two great curved trunks of oak sprang up to meet each other, and the constant thrust where they met gave the end wall its massive strength, and supported the timbers of the roof. You felt, somehow, that the house was still growing.

They had all taken to the place, were drawn to it, each for their own reasons; but of course there was no chance of them living there. Dad was tied by his job at Gemell and Hamptons. Beamsters would have to be sold.

Now, in the Beamsters garden, Cathy walked over the springy turf of the wide lawn on which old John Marshall had planted specimen trees—lime, acacia, weeping beech, showing their delicate silhouettes in the dusk— and set off down the paved walk where rosebushes, exuberant and unpruned, tumbled across the stones. She came to the new fence. When they had come the first time to see the house, she had been surprised to find the fence, thrust across the walk like a frontier, and had seen that on the other side the rosebushes had been cut back and were growing in an orderly fashion. Where the walk ended, a bright new bungalow perched upon the lawn: too new to have settled into the landscape, and in complete contrast to the weathered old house. Cathy found herself quite unreasonably offended to see it there. The ground on which it stood was obviously once part of the same garden, and must have belonged to Dad's great-uncle John. Why would he have allowed such an eyesore to be built there? It wasn't just that it was an ugly building: it was so at odds with its surroundings. But whoever lived there were the Marshalls' nearest neighbors.

For a moment Cathy paused in her speculation and saw that the Beamsters windows were lit now, and that someone had a fire going. She saw the faint shape of her father emerging from a shed with an armful of logs. He and Mum were really in their element. He had been as pleased as a dog with two tails when he had come home and told them how he had managed to arrange things so that they could live at Beamsters. Her own feelings had been very mixed. She was used to where they lived: there would be things and people she would miss. She knew very little about living in the country: she might be lonely, or bored, or even afraid. Yet there was something about that house. It would be all right, living there, even if it did take a while to grow accustomed to it.

Anyway, it seemed that at the sight and opportunity of Beamsters, Dad had decided that, after years sitting at a desk at Gemell and Hamptons dealing with paperwork about farm equipment and milking machines and feedstuffs for animals, with never a cow or a sheep or a green field in sight, he had had quite enough. Now, Joe Marshall was not a rash man, but he had gone to his boss with an idea that Cathy thought was little short of genius. They would live at Beamsters. Joe would keep Gemell and Hamptons' machinery and equipment on display there, travel around to local farms demonstrating it and giving advice, and perhaps rear a few cattle of his own on the firm's concentrates, to show how good they were.

"I'd be a rural agent," he said. "Right on the farmer's doorstep."

"Sounds like a rustic spy!" Cathy laughed.

"I'll get out my cloak and dagger," her father said. "Would you mind, though? If you would, you must say so, and I'll sell Beamsters and take the pair of you around the world on the proceeds instead."

"Oh, Joe," said Mrs. Marshall, a dreamy expression on her face as she contemplated the idea. "I could keep some hens, couldn't I?"

They had both of them looked at Cathy then. What could she say? She still had her doubts, but not about her answer.

"It's OK by me," she said. "When are we going to move?"

So they had sold their little town house and packed up their things, and Cathy had sat on the stairs at the last minute surrounded by a huddle of anonymous bundles and boxes. She knew there was no coming back, and she had felt as lumpish and heavy as the rest of the luggage.

She was growing really cold now, and there was obviously no chance that she would catch sight of their neighbors in the bungalow. There was very little point in continuing to stare at it. Deliberately she turned her back and began to walk toward Beamsters, toward the welcoming light from the kitchen. She reached up to the latch of the door, and went in.

Two

When morning came, Cathy had to push away the twigs of a plum tree before she could open her bedroom window and look down on the garden below. The twigs were whippy and vigorous, and the buds were just beginning to swell on them. In the seeming deadness of the garden there was a scattering of snowdrops, and under the acacia trees there were crocuses, in brilliant sunshiny yellow. The air was damp and cold, and smelled of the February earth.

Dad was out digging already, pleased as a kid with a new toy. He looked up at her when she called out to him, and grinned as wide as a barn door and said, "You look like Anne of Green Gables, or the Princess in the Tower. Why don't you come down and look at our flowers: they're popping up all over the place."

Cathy dressed quickly, went down to the kitchen, giving her mother a quick peck of a kiss in passing, and went out into the cool garden, where she and her father walked about on a tour of inspection, as proud as a couple of old squires inspecting their acres. Cathy still had her anxieties, but she did not mean to let anyone see them. For the moment it was good just to walk about on such a morning, breathing sweet air and getting a good appetite for breakfast. So when her father asked her if she was glad they had come, she was able to give him a good resounding "Yes!" that seemed to satisfy any last anxieties he might have had on the subject.

"Your mum and me, we've always wanted to come back to the country, you know. When I first started with Gemell and Hamptons it was only to tide me over till I could get a job on the land. Then you arrived, and I got offered a promotion, and it seemed silly to turn down good money just when we most needed it, so I stuck to the job. 'To it,' mind you, not 'with it.' Don't go thinking I've had my nose to the wrong grindstone all these years, but this—well, it's a challenge, isn't it?"

He strode on, and Cathy walked with him, along the wet, paved walk, splattering themselves with water drops as overhanging twigs brushed their heads in passing. He was filled with cheerful enthusiasm, and Mum was content with the prospect of hens to raise and a good clean drying place for the washing and fresh vegetables from the garden. But Cathy, not without despondency, wondered what this place might offer to satisfy her. What she had seen she liked, but there was too much emptiness. When she was little she used to go to the top of the road on Saturday afternoons to wait for her friend Jenny to come to tea. If Jenny was a long time coming she would play a game to herself: If the next thing that comes around the corner is a bus or a truck, I'll go home. If it's a car or a van I'll stay. If it's a motorbike I'll try again. It was rather like that now: waiting to see what would come next.

Joe Marshall was speaking to her, but she had not heard him.

"What did you say?"

"I said I'm hungry and I should think you are too. Let's go in for breakfast."

"OK."

They turned along the line of the new fence across the rose walk. Cathy thought she heard the door of the next-door bungalow slam, but though she looked carefully she could see no one there. She felt very curious to know who their neighbors were, but as yet they had not appeared, and neither Mum nor Dad knew anything about them.

Back in the Beamsters kitchen, though, Cathy found her mother inspecting a basket of eggs and reading a note that had obviously arrived with them.

"Look," Mrs. Marshall said, "aren't they beauties? Such a dark brown, and look at the size of them!"

"Who sent them?" Cathy asked.

"The note says, 'Mark and I hope you will enjoy these for breakfast. Yours, Janet Anderson (next door). P.S. We are away for the next two weeks, leaving at the crack of dawn so won't disturb you. Hope to meet when we return. Welcome to Beamsters.'

"I found the basket down by the side of the doorstep. Wasn't that kind of her?" Mrs. Marshall began to put the eggs away in the refrigerator.

"Yes," said Cathy. It didn't alter her opinion of that awful bungalow though. Well, she'd have to contain her curiosity about their new neighbors for another two weeks. Mark and Janet Anderson. She wondered if there were any children. She hoped that, if there were, they would be of a decent age: not little kids to pester her with "Will you come and play?" like the Thompson kids at home. No, not at home. This was home. Remember that. It was ridiculous that, despite the awfulness of the Thompson children, she felt a hot prickling at the back of her eyes for a moment.

Before long, however, there was so much to do that Cathy had little time to brood either over herself or her new neighbors. There was the house to clean and set to rights, and all their possessions to arrange or to store away in the ample closets the old place seemed to have in abundance. Someone, at some time in its history, had made these by the very simple method of slapping an oaken door across any nook or corner space that did not seem to fulfill any other useful function. The more Cathy lived in the house, the more it fascinated her. It was so old; yet words like "quaint" or "old world" could in no way be applied to it. It was by all modern standards as inconvenient as could be, yet it was as easy to live in as a favorite shoe. Her own room, she felt, was the best in the house, with the ribs of the roof all showing among the plaster. The dormer window had a sill so wide that to see the view all around, you had to lie flat on your stomach along it.

Now that the room was full of her own things she began to feel a little less lost in this new life. She had her record player and her tape recorder and all her books; her glass animals and the Snoopy posters she'd been given last birthday, a framed photograph of Skip and another of herself and some friends in the school play, and of course, Thred. Thred had once been known as Fluffy Bear, in the dim and distant past when Cathy had first owned him. Now he was Thred Bear. His name was a silly Cathy joke, but, as a joke, she could allow herself to keep him and she couldn't imagine life without him.

[10]

She would have to start school soon, she supposed. She had been allowed a few days' grace though, to buy her uniform and also to acquire a bicycle as there were no buses and it was too far to walk; so all three of the Marshalls felt in holiday mood, although they were so busy. Whenever there was a moment free from house arranging and digging, and the buying of paint and seeds and school blouses, they set off together to explore the grassy paths that led off in all directions into the forest, walking for miles under the still-leafless trees. The horse-chestnut buds were stickily fattening: they would be the first to brave it, and the clumps of primrose leaves hid the first few early flowers. A few days of sunshine would unfurl them in their thousands.

Before long, Joe Marshall began to take delivery of the farm machinery he was to display: a graveled yard to one side of the house and the huge barn that ran along one side of it seemed just right for this. The machinery was bright-colored, gaudy stuff, gleaming with paint in yellow and red and blue: balers, seed drills, tedders, machinery of all kinds, and sample bags of fertilizers, and sacks of feed to be stored away in big, galvanized bins. Some of the feedstuffs would be for sale, but some was for the cattle that Mr. Marshall was to buy and rear. He was really excited by the prospect of going along to the market to bid for them, yet nervous too, for he had no wish to make a fool of himself. Fortunately, he had met up with Jeff Roberts, the farmer whose cattle had previously grazed the field, in the local pub, and he had mentioned he'd be going to market that day too. No offer of help was actually made, but by the end of the evening there was a tacit understanding that Jeff would help steer Joe along the right lines where bullocks were concerned, and would stand near to him during the auction.

[11]

On the first Wednesday in March, the day of the sale, Cathy would have liked to have gone with her father, but her mother said it was best to let the two men go on their own.

"Then your dad can lean on his stick and scratch pigs' backs over the pen rails with the rest of them, and talk crops over a pint of beer with Mr. Roberts, and kid everyone he's been buying cattle from way back. Mind you, he knows what he's talking about anyway. It's just that for him it's always been on paper; never real. He's enjoying himself so much now, Cath, and it does me good to see it. I'll tell you what, though; you and I will go next week and have a look around the stalls, and buy some pullets and a cockerel, so we can have our own brown eggs, like the ones that Mrs. Anderson gave us. All right?"

"All right." Then, after a pause, "They'll be back soon, won't they? Next door, I mean."

"Yes. I suppose they will."

Cathy fell to wondering again, until her mother pushed a paintbrush into her hand and suggested they get on with redecorating the bathroom. It was a downstairs bathroom, which had seemed very strange to Cathy at first, especially as it did not look like a bathroom at all, with its steep ceiling and beamed walls. It was under the long, sloping roof at the back of the house, and its window was a pane of clear glass set into this roof, so that you could lie in the bath and look straight out into the greenness of their own patch of woodland. Clear glass took some getting used to, but she was beginning to enjoy being able to watch the birds on the branches outside, and the squirrels skittering nervously about, or sitting suddenly stock-still with their bright eyes alert and their small paws clutched to their chests. That

[12]

morning, while she was washing, a wood mouse had braved it across the window frame, its nervous, questioning whiskers brushing the glass as it darted along.

The walls of the room were stained and dark, so it was pleasant to spread the clean yellow paint over them. The rest of the house was to be white, once they had rid the walls of the odd assortment of wallpapers that had been slapped on them over the years, but this little room was the only one that turned its back on the sun, and Jean Marshall felt it needed cheering up. Cathy wondered if her mother had any feelings similar to her own about Beamsters. Was it just a lovely, unexpected gift of a house that would let her realize her dream of being a country woman again after all these years, or did she feel that there was something particular and special about it? What it was Cathy herself could not define. There was no nonsense of its being haunted. Something far more subtle than ghosts gave Beamsters that quality of being special. It seemed to contain within itself all its own past like a secret drawer in an old chest.

"Oh, what nonsense," Cathy told herself. "Get on with the painting." But it was only to her outer, practical, paintbrush-wielding self that it seemed nonsense. To her inner self it was a fact and a comfort.

Cathy was just beginning to feel hungry enough to stop and offer to make some sandwiches, when there was a knock on the front door, and still splattered and measled with paint, she went to answer it. A youngish woman, with a pleasant, smiling face, was waiting on the doorstep. As she looked at Cathy, and at the state of her, the smile widened.

"You've been busy," she said. "I'm sorry to disturb you, but I came to ask if you could all come to tea on Saturday. I'm Janet Anderson, from the bungalow."

[13]

"How do you do," Cathy said. "Come in, will you? Mum's in the kitchen, I think. She was very pleased with the eggs you sent. Thanks."

"That was nothing. They lay too many for the two of us to eat, and Mrs. Parkin, who feeds them when we're away, can't eat eggs at all."

Cathy fetched her mother, and while the two women talked, she went back to the bathroom to put the lid on the paint pot and the brushes into a jar of turpentine. Dad was very particular about tools, though in general he was the least fussy of men. She wondered how he was getting on at the market. Now, she supposed, she'd better go and be polite to Mrs. Anderson. So, it seemed there were only two of them next door, so that put an end to the possibility of there being children. She had half hoped for someone near her own age. She'd make friends at school, probably, but friendships would not be so easy, she felt, where people lived so far from each other: it wasn't like having them on the same street, or just a short walk away.

She sighed briefly, and went along to the kitchen, where her mother had, predictably, made Mrs. Anderson a cup of tea. When Cathy looked again at their new neighbor's face she saw that it was not as young a face as she had first thought, and there were lines on it that showed it was by no means always smiling. Mrs. Marshall was asking if the holiday had been a pleasant one.

"Not altogether, I'm afraid. Mark wasn't feeling too grand some of the time."

"What a shame," Cathy's mother said. "I know what it's like. My Joe had a terrible cold last time we went to Penzance, and he was in real misery. Is your husband all right now?"

"My husband?" Janet Anderson looked puzzled. Then

she said, "Oh, no! My husband died some years ago. Mark is my son. I should think he's a year or two older than Cathy. He's—Well, I'll leave him to tell you all about himself when you meet. He hates me to discuss him behind his back. You'll see him on Saturday if not before. Thanks for the tea, Mrs. Marshall."

She went out by way of the kitchen door and along the walk in the direction of the boundary fence, turning to wave good-bye at a halfway point.

"She seems nice enough," Jean Marshall remarked. "Isn't it strange how we all assumed Mark was her husband? Ah well, it'll be just right for you, won't it, a handsome young lad next door."

"Oh, Mum, really!" Cathy said. "He's probably horrible. She sounded really quite nervous when she was talking about him. He's probably got buck teeth and warts with hairs in them."

"Sounds charming," Mrs. Marshall said. "Let's hope we're in for a pleasant surprise on Saturday."

Just then Joe Marshall arrived back from town, to say he had bought half a dozen store cattle, Hereford cross Friesian, and that Jeff Roberts' cowman would bring them over in the truck when he'd delivered the animals his boss had bought for himself. Cathy was quite disappointed not to be able to view their beasts immediately, and her father roared with laughter when she told him so.

"Did you expect I'd herd them all the way back here with a stick and a dog?" he asked. "It's a goodish step from the town, you know, and mostly down the main road. I wouldn't have been any too popular, would I? Never mind, there's something for you and Mum in the car. I'll just go and fetch it."

In a short while he returned to the kitchen carrying

a large, rather flimsy-looking cardboard box with holes in it. It was making a very strange noise.

"Here you are, Jeannie, my love," he said, plonking the box into her arms. "What you've always wanted."

Cathy's mother opened the box, and inside it, like so many lively, yellow powder puffs, cheeped two dozen day-old chicks, with round, black, beady eyes, and shell-like beaks scarcely hardened as yet. She looked at them with an expression of mingled delight and exasperation.

"Joe Marshall," she said. "What on earth am I to do with these? I've no brooder to warm them, and nowhere ready to keep them. It was grown birds I was thinking of, not little baby creatures like these."

She turned around on him, and a great broad grin creased up his face in delighted triumph.

"I've got you a brooder too," he said. "I'm not daft, you know."

"Oh," she said, trying hard to continue cross, "oh"— but her face was beginning to smile in spite of herself. "Well, you'd better get it set up then, hadn't you?"

Cathy and Mr. Marshall took the chicks off to establish them in their new home.

"There's some chicken mash in the barn," Joe said. "So they won't starve, and they'll be as warm as toast under the brooder. Not just a pretty face, am I, our Cath?"

"No you're not. And I don't think Mum really minds that they're so tiny," Cathy said.

"Not she!" Her father chuckled. "These'll be the best-cared-for birds in the county, just you wait and see."

Three

At the beginning of the following week, Cathy would start school. Her uniform, blue and gold, and not too awful as uniforms go, was all bought and marked, and the bicycle had arrived from Williams' cycle shop. She had never had a new bike before, but Dad said if she was to ride it every day to school and back she needed a good machine. She had just finished pedaling it about to get the feel of it when she saw Mrs. Anderson walking across toward the back door of the bungalow with an enormous load of washing in a basket. It had been a good blowy morning and the sheets and towels had already danced themselves dry on the line. The branches of the trees were stirring and tossing too, but in the sheltered places of the garden the early spring sun was warm and pleasant.

Cathy got off her bike and walked toward the boundary fence. On the far side of the bungalow garden there was a clump of low shrubs, and she thought she caught a glimpse of a boy sitting in the shelter of them, enjoying the sunshine. She called but no one answered: she must be out of earshot. The boy did turn though, but it was only to wave to Mrs. Anderson as she walked the last few yards to the door with the washing basket. He might give her a hand, Cathy thought, virtuously. She'll never open the door loaded up like that. More to show him up than from any real motive of helpfulness, she swung over the fence and ran across the grass to open the kitchen door.

"I hope you didn't mind me coming over. I thought you looked as if you needed a hand."

"That's kind of you, Cathy. Come in, dear. Perhaps you'd help me fold the sheets. It's so much easier with two. Then perhaps you'd like to go into the garden and introduce yourself to Mark. He's at a bit of a loose end this morning."

Cathy began to help fold the sheets. Used to her own chores at home, she was quick to notice the empty coal hod by the stove, some firewood waiting to be chopped; and thought how Dad would "loose-end" him if Mark were *his* son. Perhaps Mrs. Anderson was one of those women who thought boys shouldn't be asked to help in the house, though one would have thought that attitude had joined the dodo. Still, there he was, sunning himself in the garden while everyone else worked. Cathy smoothed a sheet with quite unnecessary vigor. Waited on hand and foot, most likely. She didn't think she was going to like Mark Anderson much.

The washing all folded, Cathy moved toward the back door, and then Mrs. Anderson called out to her, "Cathy, by the way—" Those stress lines were deep in her face again, and something was making her anxious, but she let her voice trail into silence. She waved Cathy on toward the door, and found a smile, but with some difficulty.

[18]

"It's nothing. Off you go, dear, and thanks for your help."

Cathy wandered across the sunlit lawn, in no hurry to meet Mark. Everywhere daffodil leaves and buds were shooting and fattening. More and more she was beginning to notice these things. Shop daffodils, stiff yellow sentinels in regimented bunches, were a world away from these. She was becoming more aware of weather, too, and not just to grumble at it. Rain meant puddles to reflect the sky, and a good smell of wet earth, rather than the stuffiness of wet raincoats on the bus and the drips from inconsiderate umbrellas. Maybe country life was winning her over. Maybe, but it had a while to go yet.

This time, when she called out to Mark where he sat in the middle of the shrubbery, he did hear her and looked up, but made no move to rise and come and meet her, so she walked on around the end of the concealing bushes to where his chair stood on a patch of flagstones that overlooked a similar view to the one the Marshalls could see from the garden at Beamsters.

Then she saw why he had not got up to meet her. His chair was a wheelchair. Then all kinds of thoughts chased at the same time through Cathy's mind, and some of them not much to her credit. She was sorry, of course, that she had misjudged him about not doing the household chores, but she did wish most heartily that Mrs. Anderson had warned her, so that she could now think of something suitable to say. As it was, she just wished to be somewhere else. She was ashamed of the fact that she did not want to be pushed into being friends with this boy. She could just hear those pleased remarks, from Mrs. Anderson, from her parents. "It will do Mark so much good to have her company." "I'm sure Cathy will be delighted."

For a moment she considered waving to him at some distance and walking briskly by as if she were on some errand. After all, she would meet this boy on Saturday, and they could talk then. She would be more used to the idea by then, wouldn't she? But then he looked up and straight at her and somehow she could not bring herself to go on past. She felt as if she had swallowed a lump of lead.

"Hello," the boy said. "I'm Mark Anderson."

"Hello," said Cathy, keeping her distance. "Have you had an accident?" Perhaps, she thought, looking for some small hope, this is a temporary thing. His expert maneuvering of the chair dampened that idea at once.

"Not what you'd call an accident. I live in this thing. Have done since I was a kid. Didn't Mother tell you? No, I suppose she wouldn't. I got mad once because she would keep telling the story of my life, and now she won't say a dicky-bird. People just have to see for themselves, like you're doing now."

Cathy was trying hard to register a suitable expression.

"For heaven's sake," he said. "You look as if you've got a stomachache. You don't have to tell me how sorry you are, you know. I'd probably bite your head off. You don't have to talk to me at all if you don't want to. It's no skin off my nose."

Cathy looked hard at him. All this had been said, not peevishly but with an abrasive candor that made Cathy realize that no one was indulging in self-pity, unless it was herself.

"I'd like to stay and talk," she said surprising herself. "I'm Cathy Marshall from next door."

"I know that," he said. "This place isn't exactly littered with girls, and mother said there was one at

[20]

Beamsters. Do you want to sit down? There's a folding chair there, or the stones look quite warm if you don't mind the ground."

Cathy sat down on the flagstones, trying to think what to say next.

"The worst part of being in this thing," Mark went on, "is that people find it so embarrassing that they either pretend I don't really exist, like a bad smell in someone's bathroom, or they treat me like one of the more sickening characters out of Dickens, which is worse. Which category do you come in?"

He paused, looked at her sitting there with her arms around her knees, and went on, "I bet when you saw me you thought—God, I'm going to be lumbered with being nice to that."

"No, I didn't," she lied, and relapsed into silence again, deliberately staring at him. He sat in his chair, his legs wrapped in a rug, his upper body small, but square, his arms resting on the chair's arms, with his hands turned inward slightly at the wrists. He looked younger than his mother had said, except for his eyes, which held a kind of challenge, but whether for himself or for her, she did not know. They were fierce, intelligent eyes, and showed his true age.

"You don't say much, do you?" He grinned. "I always say too much. You really don't have to feel obliged to be friends unless you want to. I'm used to this, you know. It's not much more difficult to live with than flat feet or sticking-out ears. I've got a thing called muscular dystrophy. Sounds nasty, doesn't it, like something you get on your vegetables. It makes me fairly useless at walking, though, which is why I need wheels, and my co-ordination goes a bit haywire sometimes and then my arms go wonky so I have to get Mother to push me,

[21]

instead of bowling myself about. This morning, I can do you a quick twiddle"—he waltzed the chair a little, to demonstrate—"but long-distance work is definitely OUT. However," he went on, "contrary to the opinion of many observers, my brain is entirely normal and I can think as straight as the next man, always supposing him to be a straight thinker. What about you? Apart from being no conversationalist, are you all there?"

Cathy was not sure how to answer this surprising question, but she supposed he meant physically, not mentally.

"I broke my nose once" was all she could come up with. She wasn't sure why she'd thought it worth mentioning.

"Did you put *that* in a wheelchair? Are you setting up in competition?"

Mark had turned his head away and his shoulders were shaking. She must have upset him and she felt very sorry. Then she realized that it was almost uncontrollable laughter that was making him shake, and there were tears of delight on his face.

"Forgive me!" he spluttered. "I've got such a stupidly productive imagination, and it was picturing your nose all bandaged up in a wheelchair with the rest of you coming along behind like someone pushing a squash in a handcart. It's a pretty funny thought."

Feeling relaxed at last, she joined him in his delighted laughter as she sat on the warm stones by his chair.

"Old Armitage says he's not going to invite me to his funeral because I'm bound to laugh," said Mark.

"Who's he?"

"He's my tutor. He comes on weekdays to give me lessons."

"That sounds posh," Cathy said, "having a tutor."

[22]

"Me a budding squire, you mean? It's nothing like that, I assure you: just one of those little luxuries laid on by the state for kids that don't fit into the usual pigeonholes."

"What are you; tumbler, fantail or blue roller?" asked Cathy and grinned at him.

"Clay!" said Mark. "You see," he said, "when you do say something, it's worth the wait!" and started to laugh again.

When their amusement subsided there was silence again between them, and they sat watching the morning. Smoke curled white out of the kitchen chimney at Beamsters where Mrs. Marshall was relighting the stove. She had not got the measure of it yet, and it still chose her busiest morning to sulk itself out. Mark watched the white drift vanish into blue, and then turned thoughtfully to Cathy.

"So," he said. "You're the girl who lives at the old house now. Well, it could be worse, I suppose."

His face was very solemn now.

"The thought seems to make you pretty gloomy," Cathy observed. "Do you really mind so much?"

"Oh, take no notice of me. It's not you I mind, it's anyone who lives at Beamsters. You see, when the house stood empty for a while I used to like pretending it was mine. I love old houses, but I have to live in a modern house because of getting this thing about." Mark patted the arm of his wheelchair. "Old houses are mostly up and downs, Beamsters more than most, and that puts paid to my wheeling about in them, but they've always been a love of mine, their histories, the feel of them, the knowledge that people have lived in them for generations. Have you any idea how long there has been a house at Beamsters?"

[23]

"I know it's very old."

"It's the oldest house in the county," Mark declared, "and there was a house on the site before William the Conqueror. There's a piece of stone in the wall that probably came from a Roman temple. Did you know that?"

"Dad showed me a stone slab, low down on the cruck wall. There are letters on it, but we could not read them. The solicitor was going to come over and tell us all he knew about the house's history, but he's been very busy."

"I can tell you all he'll know and more too," Mark said. "I used to talk to old Mr. Marshall whenever he felt up to it, and I've studied books and parish records and tombstones and goodness knows what, to find out about Beamsters. Why didn't you ever come here when the old man was alive?"

"I never knew about him," Cathy said, "and Mum and Dad are so close and so taken up with each other I suppose they never thought to keep contact with him. I'm sorry now. It seems a shame when he's given us all this."

"Well," said Mark, "if he can hear that I think he'll forgive you! He was a nice old chap. But I was telling you about the stone in the wall. It must have been there in the original house—or one of the original houses. They were always getting burned down and rebuilt in those days, you know."

"What do the letters on the stone say?"

"I think it's ECCE, the Latin for 'look' or 'behold' or what have you, and there's a D too, so it could possibly be ECCE DEUM, 'behold the god,' which seems quite likely if it came from a temple."

"It could have been DEAM, 'behold the goddess,'" remarked Cathy.

"Don't quibble," Mark reproved her. "Whoever put the stone in the wall must have had courage, though.

[24]

Most of the Saxons thought there was evil magic in the old Roman buildings, and would leave them well alone, but then, when you think whose house it was, I suppose they thought a little magic wouldn't do any harm."

"Whose house was it, then?" asked Cathy.

"Why, the Beemaster's house, of course. Didn't you know that either? That's the meaning of its name."

"I thought the name was because of the great timbers in the walls and the roof. I never thought of bees. Why should bees be so important that the house should keep the name of the Beemaster after all these hundreds of years?"

Mark looked at her with a mixture of pity and amusement.

"You don't know anything, do you?" he asked. Then, apologetically, "I'm sorry, that was rude of me. It's just that it's such a hobby of mine that I assume everyone else must be just as interested."

"I *am* interested," Cathy assured him, "but you're quite right, I don't know much about the house yet, and I never was much good at history."

"I don't think *I'm* much good at what most people think of as history. Politics and treaties and dates of kings are like so much cold mutton fat as far as I am concerned, but anything that's happened to real people in real places in the past fascinates me. Then my mind likes to embroider it with colors and patterns from my own imagination, and stories write themselves in my head. I used to write them down, but since my arms went wonky I haven't been able to write very quickly. I could do with one of those typewriters you blink at, but I can't see me getting one. I've got a story ready to write now, about how the first house was built at Beamsters, but I'll just have to wait till Mother's got time to hear it and type it for me, and by then I'll have forgotten half the things I wanted to say. Mother's always so darned busy."

He hunched himself into silence until Cathy felt he could well have forgotten she was there. What an extraordinary boy he was. Wheelchair or no wheelchair, she told herself, she had never met anyone quite like this before.

An idea occurred to her: she hoped it would be a useful one.

"I've got a tape recorder," she said. "You could use that if you like. You could dictate bits as you think of them until you've finished the story, and then your mother could type it out whenever she could spare the time and nothing would get forgotten."

Mark looked at her as if she'd performed some astounding conjuring trick, and he could not quite believe it.

"You're a marvel," he said. "The moment you see me your face falls a mile and you look as though you'd like to run away, and now here you are, offering me good ideas and tape recorders. What did the trick then?"

She hadn't realized how obvious she'd been. It was as if he could read her thoughts.

"I like living in Beamsters," she said, in explanation, "and you seem to know all about it. There are things I'd like to know, too."

She could not explain to him how she felt about the place, but she was sure he felt the same.

"I'd better go now," she said. "I'll bring the recorder and some blank tapes over when we come to tea tomorrow." She studied his face for a moment, and added, "Or sooner, if you like?"

"Sooner, please." He was smiling, but the expression

[26]

had something less comfortable than a smile. Cathy knew what it was like to have ideas tunneling in the brain like moles and no way of trapping them. Ideas elusive as dreams must be caught before they vanished.

"I'll be back in a jiff," she said.

She leaped to her feet, vividly aware of the strength in her legs, and ran off toward the house.

"Thanks!" he called after her.

Four

Before they went across to tea the next day, Cathy decided she ought to warn her mother about Mark. Mrs. Marshall's swift compassion for any creature's misfortune could well, Cathy felt, be misinterpreted, so it was best to set her right on the matter.

"For heaven's sake, don't look *sorry* for him, will you, Mum? He doesn't like pity."

"There's nothing wrong with pity, our Cath," her mother said; "it's how you show it that matters. But don't worry, I shan't upset him."

Joe Marshall had had to go to Bucklehurst to deliver a tractor, so he did not accompany them, but Janet Anderson was quick to welcome the other two Marshalls and invite them into the sitting room, which had a wide window overlooking an expanse of green turf and flower beds.

"The bungalow's called 'Lawn End,' by the way," Mrs. Anderson said. "Though I've never bothered with a name board. I love the outlook from this window. Even Mark had to admit it's one of the advantages of a modern house that you get a good clear view from a window like this, without mullions and transoms and lattices and so on. By the way, Cathy, it was so kind of you to lend Mark your tape recorder: he's been really cheerful all day. I should have thought of it myself, of course, but I don't get to Bucklehurst much, and I've been busy getting straight after the holiday. I just wish it had done him more good, but it wasn't a great success, what with his being ill, and then something happening to depress him that I still haven't been able to discover. It's not easy."

This was a statement, rather than a complaint, but Mrs. Anderson looked despondent herself, until Mark came in, self-propelled, though with obvious effort, and she altered her face to a deliberate cheerfulness. He got to his place, though Cathy could see his arms weren't doing as he asked them, and they all sat down to tea and toast and homemade cake. It was an uncomfortable meal. Mark had obvious difficulty in getting his food to his mouth and Cathy was on tenterhooks in case her mother should say or do something unwise.

Later, the two women went off to look over the house, and Cathy and Mark were left to each other's company. Cathy's tenseness eased a little.

"I've got the beginnings of something on tape that I'd like you to hear," Mark said, full of enthusiasm. Then, hesitating, "If you want to, that is."

"Yes, I do. Can I take it home and play it, and bring it back tomorrow?"

"That would be fine. And thanks, Cathy. I'm glad you've come here, even though it does mean I can't pretend Beamsters is mine anymore."

"Mum says it's not the sort of house that belongs to people: they belong to it. Anyway, your house is in part of the old garden, and your roses are on the same walk as the Beamsters ones. When you used to visit Great-uncle John, how did you manage to get about inside the house, with all the steps and angles?"

"He used to carry me." Mark grinned. "He was a fair-sized man, and strong, even if he *was* old."

"Dad's used to carrying feed bags. I should think he could manage you," said Cathy. "So that's all right, isn't it? And anyway, no one can stop you living where you like, in your imagination, now can they? Your mind can live where it chooses."

She shut her mouth then, firmly. It was the sort of remark that among her friends would cause them to give her that look that meant "Cathy Marshall's a bit odd, you know."

Mark said, "All right then, I'll take up mental residence at once, and if you feel you're being haunted, it will only be me."

As she sat in her room that evening, getting the recorder ready to play back Mark's tape, she chuckled to herself, remembering that remark, and tried to imagine him, in traditional ghostly guise, floating about near the ceiling and wafting in the draft from the window. Then the tape began to speak, and she settled down to listen. She had no idea what to expect: how he would set about describing what he knew of the history of the old house. What she heard, in Mark's voice, breathy but unmistakable, was a fabric of fact and invention, his own story of how Beamsters may have begun.

"There was a clearing in the trees where the common shouldered its way into the forest, where the young oaks had flourished in the extra light. Their branches overhung the tussocky grass, shedding acorns for the grateful pigs and dead wood for the old women who came gathering for the fire, by hook or by crook, as the custom was. The oak leaves were edged and splotched with brown now, for the summer was waning and the cattle were grazing the stubble of the village fields.

"The rooting pigs suddenly scattered, as a man approached, an axe on his shoulder, its blade gleaming in the sun as he walked against the strong light, shading his eyes from it with his hand. As he came nearer the forest the great trees blocked the sun and plunged him into the blue-green of their shadows, through which the insistent rays pierced like rods and bars of gold. As he entered, a few deer, dappled like the forest floor, melted silently away at this invasion of their private place, and a magpie scolded him roundly.

"The man unslung a bag from his shoulder and leaned his axe against one of the oaks, before walking slowly from tree to tree, gazing at each appraisingly, tapping the trunk and studying its whole length from roots to topmost twig until he seemed to arrive at a conclusion. He picked up the axe again and set its edge to the base of his chosen tree. He was humming a tune to himself and scattering a few words to it here and there:

Mischief take the hazel tree,
Oak's the only wood for me.

Then the haft and head of the axe were drawn back in a great arc and swung again to bite into the wood, leaving a yellow cleft mark from the one iron tooth on the young smoothness of the bark. The great old trees, safe by reason of their girth from the man's small axe, sighed through all their branches as the edge bit again. In this way was cut the first tree for the timbers of the Beemaster's house."

[31]

The recorder went on spinning out Mark's words, and Cathy listened in the growing dusk, until at last the voice clicked into silence.

When she slept that night, she dreamed that all the timbers of the house had put out leaf and branch and become part of the dark and tangled forest, with wolf voices not far off, and little rough thatched huts huddled together in the clearing. It was a wild, uncomforting place, and she was glad to wake out of it. She was glad for the Beemaster too, that his house was framed with oak.

When she went to take the machine back to tell Mark how much she'd enjoyed his story, she found him drooping and low-spirited.

For a long time he sat glumly and spoke only in monosyllables, making her feel so awkward that she could scarcely think of anything to say either. At last he found his voice, though, and having looked hard at her, said, "Cathy, suppose one morning you woke up and the whole world knew how to fly except you; really fly, with wings I mean; and you watched them all take to the air and climb and stoop and soar like so many eagles, and only you were left with your feet in the mud. How would you feel?"

"Horrible," said Cathy. "So horrible, I couldn't tell you."

"Well, that's how I feel a lot of the time. People who are whole have this trite belief they comfort themselves with, that if you're disabled you're always brave and uncomplaining, and don't really miss being ordinary. 'Isn't he marvelous, Mrs. Anderson?' they say. 'All things considered, and what a credit to your sacrifice,' et cetera, et cetera, as if I were a clever dog performing tricks. Sometimes, Katy-cat, there's enough resentment in me to split the whole world at the seams."

Cathy saw the fierce eyes looking at her from that bleak face and felt desperately uncomfortable. There was nothing to say that would not sound false and trite. She knew she must make him talk again though, for she guessed he seldom spoke to people as he had just spoken to her. It was an odd sort of honor, and very much a burden, too.

She seized on the strange name he had called her, as a way of altering the subject without changing it.

"No one's ever called me that before: 'Katy-Cat.' I'm Cathy, or Catherine at school, or even Kitty sometimes, or Mum calls me Cath, but that's a new one."

"Do you mind it?"

"No. It's odd, though."

"Well, so are you. Nice odd. You sat by the fire yesterday, all quiet and relaxed like a cat by the hearth, and it was good to watch you. You mustn't mind me, you know. I'm not trying anything on. I wouldn't get far if I was, would I?"

The humor came back into his eyes, and began to alter the downward pull of his mouth.

"You're OK, Katy-Cat, really you are, and you comfort me. I get scared sometimes, and I need someone to talk to who isn't going to get fussed the way Mother does. I suppose she thinks I'll die and leave her on her own."

He scowled again. "I'm not scared of death, you know," he said, "though I can't help hoping some miracle cure

[33]

might fly in through a window like old Fleming's penicillin."

He paused, and looked at Cathy as if waiting for her to interpose some remark, and when she did not, he grinned in earnest, and said, "Thank God you didn't twitter when I talked about dying. It's a forbidden subject you know, like sex behind the bicycle sheds. People do it, but they don't let on."

"There's no point in worrying about dying," Cathy said cheerfully, "After all, you could be run over by a bus tomorrow."

"I'd have to try quite hard," said Mark.

"I could always push you, you know," Cathy threatened, and grabbed the wheelchair as if to carry out the threat on the instant.

For a while she kept him cheerful, but she could see it was hard going for him. His mother had explained to Cathy that there were patches when he felt a great deal better, but they only made his overall increasing weakness more depressing. "He has to live more and more in his mind," she had said, "and thank goodness he has such imagination and is clever with words. Still, there's something particularly amiss with him at the moment, and I just cannot fathom what it is."

Cathy, aware that he had told her a great deal of himself already, plunged boldly in after that one.

"Is there anything specially wrong?" she asked.

"Or just self-pity, you mean? More than that, though that comes into it. It was those damned horses."

It was such a surprising answer, especially given with such vehemence—and one that was not really an answer at all because it brought its own obvious question with it—that she stared at him with her mouth open.

"You look like a fish," he said. " 'What horses?' you are about to ask."

"I wasn't. I just hoped you'd tell me."

"I'll tell you. When we were away on holiday, Mother took me to a place called Chalgrove Hall. It wasn't her idea. Miss Barnes, the physiotherapist, knew about it, and told her to take me. They do riding there for people like me."

"Riding for the Disabled," said Cathy. "We collected for it at school."

"Bully for you," Mark said, unimpressed. "Off we set, Mother and me, and watched all these kids riding in a big indoor place: spastics, thalidomides, all sorts, and getting about all over the place on ponies. Mind you, they'd have had a hard job to fall off with all the people there were to help. They were having no end of a good time. Then one of the people running it came up and asked Mother if I'd like to try it. Well, I wasn't really keen because I've never had much to do with horses, and Mother worries about everything on principle, but the chap seemed so confident and persuaded her so much that I'd enjoy it that they had me wheeled up onto a sort of platform ready for takeoff before I could say very much. They put a great leather belt around me so they could hold on to me, and stuck one of those silly hats on my head, and up came a little rusty-colored horse with a saddle on it with a big handle in the front. There was a girl on it: about eight or nine I should think, and when they asked her to let me have a turn she hopped off with no trouble at all, and it wasn't until she was on the ground holding the handrail you could see she had one useless leg.

"They patted the horse all over so I could see it was

[35]

quiet, and then they heaved and shoved and steadied me until I was sitting on its back holding on to the handle. Then they led me around."

"You obviously can't have enjoyed it much," Cathy observed. "It certainly seems to have upset you."

"Upset me?" he glared at her, clenching and unclenching his hands as they lay in his lap, "Don't you realize that for the first time that I can really remember I was moving about without wheels? I had those wings I was telling you about: just for five minutes I was free. I was really free. I wish I'd never done it, and then I'd never have known how it felt. Oh, it's no good. I can't explain. I must sound like a kid howling for a lost toy. It's more than that, honestly it is."

He stared down at his hands, his whole body shrunken up with misery, and his eyes were very bright.

"I know that, stupid," Cathy said, briskly annoyed with herself for having got the wrong idea. "It can't be impossible, surely, to do the same thing around here. Have you tried?"

"There's nowhere," he said. "Except Crosskeys Stables; all very snobby and run by the horsiest pair of women you've ever seen. We went there to watch my cousin Angela have a riding lesson when she deigned to visit us last year. She hates me. I don't blame her. I'm always rude to her. She thinks anyone who doesn't know about withers and fetlocks and what have you must be a cretin. That's going to be one of my troubles, isn't it? I want to ride but I can't bear horsey people. I don't even know if I like horses much: I've had very little to do with them. But I want that freedom again, Cathy: I really do."

Cathy knew something of what he felt. After all, she

had not known, with any certainty, whether she was going to like living in the country. Certain aspects of it worried her a good deal: yet now she realized, rather to her surprise, that if someone were to take her forever from this new life, she would be heartbroken.

"Leave it with me," she said. "I'll have a think about it."

She hoped there was some confidence in her voice.

"Come on: I'll take you up into the forest."

It was a poor substitute for what he was longing for, but for the moment it was better than nothing.

She pushed him out through the wide door of the bungalow and they set off toward the timber track that went for miles into the forest, and was smooth enough for the wheelchair even at this time of year when the other paths were miry and rutted.

Out in the air he began to brighten a little, and his humor returned. One of the things that she was growing to like most in him was that even from the depths he could see flashes of how comic life was: ridiculous sometimes. Good for a laugh, anyway. Now he gathered up reins from his lap and cracked an imaginary whip in the crisp air.

"Wagons Ho!" he shouted, and she broke into a co-operative canter, so that the chair trundled on with some speed among the trees. The wind had been blustery since early morning, and it roared above their heads in the trees, clashing branch on branch in an exhilarating spring blow. It took Cathy's breath away as she labored up a slope with the chair, her pace slackening and her cheeks pink with effort. Mark looked over his shoulder toward her.

"And does the road wind uphill all the way?" he declaimed, bellowing into the buffeting air. "Yes! To the very end."

"Not quite," puffed Cathy, "only to Rook's Cross. And if you go on like that you can freewheel all the way down again." Her legs were aching. Her back hurt. She felt sure she was not altogether joking.

"You wouldn't . . ." he said. " 'It is a far far worse thing that you do now . . .' "

"I warned you," Cathy spluttered, her humor returning and made as if to turn the chair and let him bowl off down the hill. He knew quite well she wouldn't. He rolled his eyes in a pretense of terror and clasped his hands as if in prayer, until Cathy relented and began the uphill push again.

At Rook's Cross they found as sheltered a place as they could, and stopped to gaze at the view: it was the garden view again but from so much higher a vantage point that one could see far greater distances both far and wide.

"It's great," Mark said, "looking at something like that. Better than food. Better than anything."

"I wish I could paint," Cathy said.

"You'd only get one instant of it then," Mark said. "Watch! It paints itself, all the time. Wind blows across it, clouds shadow it. Smoke from those chimneys swirls into shapes. There's sun on that hill, but in a moment it will be on the next, and that one will be dark brown plowland instead of the bright gold it is now."

Cathy was silent, watching. At last she said, "I suppose we'd better get back."

It seemed a damping, practical sort of remark on such

[38]

a day and in such a place, but Mark agreed cheerfully enough.

"We'll come again." he said.

On the way back Cathy talked to him about the tape he had made.

"I liked it. You should do a lot more. Dad might help type for you if your mother's too busy. It's good stuff, Mark—you ought to get it published. I think it's smashing."

She had no idea if a publisher would consider it, but she knew she had enjoyed every word. Mark had his doubts.

"Who'd want to read my meanderings?" he asked. "I like to get my ideas down, to stop them buzzing about in my head, but no one else would be interested."

"I am," Cathy said.

He grinned at her. "You're not just anyone. You're Katy-Cat, and you're crackers anyway. Otherwise you wouldn't put up with me."

"You're crackers too, then," she countered. "All the best people are crackers. They're the people to write for. The others don't read anything but the *Football Quarterly*, or the *Financial Times*, or . . . or the *Squirrel Breeders' Gazette*. If you really read, you've got to want to live for a while in someone else's imagination, and believe it to be true and real in the proper sense of true and real. And you've got an imagination worth living in."

Cathy paused. She had not meant to say all that. She had never given such things very much thought before.

"Wow," said Mark, having looked at her for some time

[39]

with his eyes wide. "For a quiet girl, you said quite a lot there, didn't you?" He sighed. "You're right, of course you are, but I'm not sure my stuff qualifies. However, push the genius home, will you, before my nose goes numb. It's you that's getting the exercise, remember. I only live here."

They set off on the downhill slope, and Cathy braced herself against it as the wheelchair's momentum tugged at her arms. They were walking into the wind now, and Mark clutched his cold nose and sang against it in an adenoidal pseudo-Brooklyn accent:

> "De sprig is sprug, de grass is riz,
> I wudder where de boidies is?
> Dey say de boid is od de wig
> But dat's absoid
> Because de wig is od de boid."

"You're incorrigible," Cathy shouted.

"No, in a wheelchair," he yelled back.

Mrs. Anderson, watching them come out of the trees in the direction of Lawn End, saw they were both convulsed with laughter—though she could hear nothing above the sound of the increasing gale—and wondered what on earth they had found so funny.

Five

During the next week Cathy was very much occupied with the touchy business of becoming accustomed to her new school. She hadn't much enjoyed starting the old one, but at least there all the new students were plunged in together. Here it was like putting your toe in the water and going in slowly. She found the long cycle ride tiring too, though it was fun bowling along the early morning road. She wondered what it would be like in winter; dark going and dark coming home. That was a long time off, though: there was a whole summer and autumn ahead of her before that: three more seasons in which to see Beamsters as she had not yet seen it. It would "paint itself," as Mark had said the whole wide landscape did, in all the different lights and aspects of the year.

The problem of Mark and the horses weighed heavily on her mind. There were girls at school who rode, but she didn't seem to think they would be helpful. Crosskeys was the only riding school for miles around, and the only horses she saw about in the fields were obviously the expensive sort one hunted on, or went to horse shows with. There were ponies in the forest, of course, but they were wild and shy, though her father assured her they all belonged to somebody. They could be seen in wary groups, their manes a tangle of burrs, their ribs showing the hard winter they had endured. She could not imagine Mark riding one of those. She wished she knew just a little more about the whole subject, or could find someone who did.

On Friday, after school, she stood with her dad by the field fence, watching the bullocks graze. The grass was just beginning to get really green. She had not realized how drab it got in the winter until this vigorous new color began to show.

The bullocks were young and woolly and wide-eyed. They would graze a little, then raise their heads to stare at the two figures leaning on the rail. One, who was the boldest, approached from time to time, full of curiosity and, with outstretched head, touched Joe Marshall's fingers with its wet nose and rough tongue. Then it backed away, snorting. The warier ones began to join in this game, until they were all playing a sort of bovine version of fox and geese.

Mr. Marshall seemed to be concentrating his attention on the game, but after a while, he said to Cathy, "There's something on your mind, my girl, isn't there? You've been thoughtful all week. Your mother thinks you're sickening for something."

She looked at him in surprise. He always knew so much more about her than she thought showed. She told him about Mark and what had happened at Chalgrove Hall. She hoped Mark wouldn't mind. Joe Marshall listened, and then went on playing with the cattle for a while. Then he said, "It sounds like a 'Do-It-Yourself' job to me."

"What do you mean?" Cathy asked.

He looked around the field consideringly, and then said, "It seems to me there's plenty of room in here for a pony."

It had never occurred to her even to think of that possibility.

"Dad, it's a lovely idea, but I don't know the first thing about ponies, and neither does Mark. I can't even ride."

"I can."

"What?"

"I learned in the Army. Mind you, I wasn't very good. But I do know a little bit, and I used to help old Milkie on his rounds when I was a kid, and he was a stickler for doing things right. I expect it would come back to me."

Cathy still had her doubts, even so. It wouldn't be like having a pony for just anyone to ride. Mark would need special treatment, special gear. All the problems inherent in her idea continued to weigh on Cathy like an unshiftable lump. Her father saw her anxious face: saw how much she wanted to get this right and not let it be just a good idea that didn't come off.

"You've got problems, Cath, but they're not impossibilities," he said. "Let's look at what you've got on your side. There's plenty of grass here, and the bullocks won't mind a bit of company, I don't suppose. There's a stable at the end of the barn that wants clearing out because it's full of old junk, and once it's empty it might as well be used. Then there's one more thing."

"What's that?"

[43]

"Under all that gloom I think you really want to do this, don't you?"

"Oh, Dad, I do."

"That's what matters, my girl. I'm going to start asking around then, at all the farms I visit, and see if there are ponies for sale around here and what the price is like."

Cathy had never got as far as thinking in terms of hard cash. The idea had not so far become that real.

Mr. Marshall went on: "Now you've put it in my mind, I think I'd like to see a pony about the place, something that could help me cart stuff around. Be interesting for customers too."

"Dad, you can't afford to buy me a pony."

"I'm not. I'm buying myself a pony. If I choose to lend it to you and Mark, that's up to me, isn't it?"

She turned to him and gave him a great hug as if she'd squeeze him to death.

"Dad, you're a dear, you really are."

"Get on with you," he said. "I've told you, coming here's the best thing that ever happened to me. Why not let someone else share the benefit? That's if the idea works, of course. There are bound to be problems. There always are."

"I know," Cathy said, wishing she hadn't such a clear picture of the pitfalls all around. For one thing, Mark would certainly be very prickly if he had the least suspicion that the pony was being bought for his benefit. Stupid, Cathy told herself. Underneath, he's bound to suspect. They must make sure that he never had to admit to it. He can know, but we mustn't make him feel we know he knows. She explained this complex piece of reasoning to her father, who roared with laughter and

[44]

said she'd get a pain in her brain if she let her thoughts get so tied up in knots.

"Just leave it to me," he assured her. "I'll make sure he knows it was all off my own bat that I did it. I'll have a word with his mother too."

Cathy began to protest.

"Don't worry," Joe Marshall said. "I'm good at handling women," and he winked at her.

She had to admit he was. She hadn't felt so cheerful for days.

It was Mum who a few days later brought Miss Barnes home to tea. She met the young woman who was Mark's physiotherapist in one of the hardware shops in Bucklehurst. They had got into conversation on the subject of saucepans, and when Miss Barnes discovered that Mrs. Marshall lived at Beamsters, she begged a lift there, as she was due to visit Mark and her car was being temperamental.

"Mrs. Anderson would run me back to the garage afterward, but it seems a waste to ask her to fetch me as you're going that way."

When they arrived at Lawn End, however, the bungalow was all locked up, and the Andersons were out: so when Cathy arrived home from school she found the tea party going on: her mother and father and a very attractive young woman. She could hardly believe it was Miss Barnes, whom Mark had described as "a real sadist—never happy unless it hurts."

"I'm glad you've come, Cath," Joe Marshall said. "I

think it would be a good thing if you talked to Miss Barnes about your idea."

Cathy looked at her and decided she could be trusted.

"You remember you suggested Mark should go to Chalgrove Hall?" Cathy asked.

"Yes, I certainly do."

Cathy explained what the riding had meant to Mark, and how desperately he wanted to do it again. Jenny Barnes listened and looked most concerned.

"I wish he'd told me. I wondered why he was so depressed. He just hasn't been trying recently."

"His mother's been worried too," Jean Marshall said. "Joe's had a word with her about it."

"And we want to do something about it too," said Joe. "Cathy's had a grand idea."

Cathy explained, adding that it was her dad's idea really: she'd just been floundering about, wanting to help. She was worried. A physiotherapist might say the whole thing was impossible, that a center like Chalgrove was the only proper place for Mark to ride; and that, so many miles away, was impossible, except as a holiday treat, a couple of times a year.

The reaction was surprising.

"It's a splendid idea. With the right help, I'm sure it could work."

Cathy could hardly believe it. Jenny Barnes was smiling with approval.

"I'll check with Dr. Wainwright, of course, but for my own part I would think that taken slowly and carefully, this could be just the right thing for Mark, and I'll be happy to help as much as I can. You'll have to make yourself realize though, Cathy, that it can't effect any sort of cure, and it may not make the least

[46]

difference to his physical state; he has a wasting disease and it's progressive. Some days are better than others, as I expect you've found out already, and if he improves after a session of riding you might be tempted to think that's the cause, but don't be. Mark hit the best and soundest reason himself. It made him feel free. Gave him a new dimension. That's what counts."

"I understand," Cathy said. She did understand, but she still had a sneaking wish that being friends with Mark had not let her in for so much that was hard to accept. Why was life so unreasonable and so unfair?

Cathy shook herself, aware that she should be listening more carefully to what the physiotherapist was saying.

"I've said I'll help, and I'll teach you all the exercises he can safely do when I'm not around, but I know someone else who might be useful to you. A friend of mine, who's quite an expert. You might get some books on riding from the library, and on how to look after ponies and so on. There's probably a great deal more to it than one thinks. There usually is!"

"Well now, there's an ally for you," Mr. Marshall said when the physiotherapist had left.

"Pretty, isn't she?" Cathy said.

"I'd walk for her if I had two broken legs," said her father, and dodged a mimic blow from his wife, who was clearing the table.

"She makes you feel confident," Jean Marshall said. "If she thinks riding will be good for Mark, then the sooner he starts the better. Have you begun looking around for a pony?"

"Not yet."

"Well, keep your mind on that, and off pretty women, Joe Marshall."

"And how am I to do that, when I'm married to one?"

Next day before she set off home after school, Cathy went into the library and asked for books about horses. The librarian showed her where to find all there were on the subject, and she tried to make her choice, though it was confusing among so many.

Some of them were obviously far beyond her, with complicated diagrams and even more complicated texts, but after a search she found one with clear photographs and a straightforward explanation of *Your Pony from A to Z*. Then she discovered a jokier one called *So You Think You Know About Horses*, with some witty sketches that she thought might amuse Mark. It seemed suitable reading, she thought, for an idiot like herself who knew nothing about horses at all, and it comforted her that the title implied that even people who thought they did might be wrong sometimes. She put these two books under her arm and was just about to head for the desk when she noticed a slim, cloth-covered book, wedged between *Finer Points of Equitation* and *The Stallion Handler's Guide*. She pulled it out, and saw that it was called *Riding with a Handicap*. It was full of pictures of disabled children and adults, riding and doing exercises on horseback. There were sketches of special saddles and reins, and of platforms and ramps for mounting from a wheelchair. It was exactly what was needed, and as she turned the pages she began to feel that, perhaps after all, she had not taken on the impossible. She felt a queer, tickling excitement inside. She wanted to get on with the job. She wanted to see Mark's face when he knew he had the chance to ride again. The library floor seemed a long way under her feet as she drifted out into the roadway to find her bicycle.

She raised the kickstand and began to ride home, her imagination working to clothe the bike's metal frame with muscle and flesh. Taking one hand from the handlebars, she patted an unseen neck, and seemed to feel warm and supple skin beneath her fingers.

When she got home, her mother was sitting at the table, scraping carrots. "We'll have our own out of the garden later on this year," she said.

Cathy showed her the books, and they looked carefully through the third one together. Mrs. Marshall made as if to speak to Cathy, hesitated, as if uncertain of her words, and then said, "Cathy, I don't want to sound like . . . I don't want you to think I'm . . ."

"Come on, Mum, what are you trying to say?" Cathy asked. She knew something must be bothering her mother. It was a sure sign when she left sentences in midair like that.

"Look, love," Mrs. Marshall said. "About Mark. You were listening to what Miss Barnes said about him, weren't you? I mean, really taking it in? If he were anyone else, we'd be teasing you, I expect, and calling him your boyfriend, but as it is . . ."

"Oh, Mum, don't look so worried. I'm not a baby anymore, but I don't want boyfriends either. Not the way you mean. Mark and I get on all right, and I'd like to help him, and I like his company. Let's just leave the rest, shall we? I'm not an ostrich. There's no sand in my eyes. Honestly."

Mrs. Marshall put her arms around her in a reassuring hug before she returned to scraping the carrots.

"All right then, Cath. We'll leave it at that. I should have known you'd have plenty of sense. Oh, by the way, Mrs. Anderson's brought over some typing she's been doing, and another tape recording. Mark's been having bad headaches these last few days, and he asked her to ask you to check the typescript against the tape. He was a bit fed up that you hadn't been in to see him the last couple of days. I said you'd had a lot on at school, and plenty of homework to get through."

"You're right there," Cathy groaned. "About six acres of French verbs and an essay on Napoleon tonight. I'd better get on with it. I'll listen to the tape afterward." I *do* have other things to do, she added to herself. He's just got to realize that. I can't spend all my time thinking about him.

There was a message for her at the beginning of the tape.

"When are you coming over? Sorry to lumber you with this, but I haven't been so good lately. I've been watching your father playing with his cows. Why not knit me a matador jacket and involve me in an exciting new hobby?" Cathy giggled, picturing the scene.

"On your advice I've written some more. Glad you liked the first part. According to the records, the man who kept bees here before the Conquest was a more than ordinary chap, which is why I gave him an oak-framed house instead of the usual hazel and daub. I should have made him talk in Anglo-Saxon, I suppose, but I'm not up to that. My father could have done it. He could quote reams of glorious stuff about Beowulf, and Byrtnoth; and reel off gloomy sayings about fate being inexorable, and man's life being like a sparrow's flight across the lit hall out of the dark night and into the dark night again.

"To get back to the bees, though, it seems that the men who looked after the bees—*beeceorls*, they were called—weren't usually particularly well thought of. They were about the lowest of the freemen and had to work hard for their lord as well as with the bees. This particular man seems to have been very highly esteemed, though, by all the others in the village. He may have been particularly skilled in beekeeping, or he may perhaps have had powers of healing, which Beemasters are often known to have. When I really get down to finishing that bit of story I'm going to try to write that in. I don't know the name of my first Beemaster, but his son is mentioned in an old manuscript they've got in a library in Oxford. His name was Edwin, and there's a really extraordinary legend attached to him, that for his sake King William let the village remain as a village and did not take it under his Forest Law. You know how fond William was of hunting, and he took great areas of land for his deer without troubling himself about who lost their livelihood and lands. No one knows the true story; but this is my version. . . .

"There was a row of six wicker hives under a lean-to roof in the most sheltered part of the Beemaster's garden, and the bees were taking instruction for their day's flight from the scouts who had already ranged far across the clearings in the forest. They knew the young man was approaching, but he was not their Beemaster, and their voices swelled to a suspicious muttering, which rose and hovered and then died down again as they saw

[51]

him stand at a respectful distance. Then he spoke to them quietly and sadly:

" 'Bees, oh bees, your master is dead, and I, Edwin his son, will care for you if you will serve me, and I will live here in the Beemaster's house, for my father served our old lord well and he has given me the house and the bees instead of taking them for himself, as his right is. Will you serve me contentedly, and give me your golden honey to pay my dues, and wax for the priest's candles, and the power to heal that you gave my father?'

"He approached the hives then, and the bees murmured quietly amongst themselves, and set out on their flights and did him no harm. He was accepted.

"From then on, whenever anything happened to please or to trouble young Edwin, he would come to the hives early in the morning, and tell his bees; and the pleasure grew and the trouble waned with the telling of it.

"But after a while King William took land from the old lords to make himself a hunting forest, dispossessing villagers all around so that livelihoods were gone and they had no work. Edwin grew anxious as the lands around his own village came under threat, and he told the bees.

" 'They say this William loves his deer as if they were his brother. I wish he had as much love for his subjects as he had for the deer.'

"One day King William came hunting in the forest near Edwin's cottage, and the hounds, holding a deer at bay, disturbed a nest of wild bees that attacked the hunting party and terrified the king's horse. It threw its rider and, in panic, gashed its shoulder on a hazel stake so that it was lamed and bleeding."

Mark's description of the poor beast was so vivid that Cathy could almost feel in herself the pain in skin and muscle, could imagine the creature sweating and blown, and William's horror at the sight of it.

"Slowly they led the horse out of the forest, and came to Edwin's house.

"Edwin had no love for this Norman who called himself the King of England, but he would let no beast suffer if he could heal it.

"Edwin looked at the wound and saw that it would take great skill to cure it.

" 'Can anything be done?' King William asked him.

"The forester, who was the King's chief servant that day, was all for despatching the horse with his long knife, but Edwin spoke up.

" 'I can cure the wound.'

" 'Speak respectfully to your King,' growled the forester.

" 'I can make the horse well,' said Edwin, 'whether he's a king's horse or drayman's. It's all one to me.'

" 'Make him well then, if you can,' said the King. 'Whose man are you?'

" 'My own man, a freeman, but I serve the lord you have set over us, and he has his dues from me, or will do while I keep my livelihood.'

"Edwin went to his store then, and brought honey and great damp leaves of broad plantain, and other herbs from the garden. He hobbled the horse tightly, but it was weak from lack of blood, and stood shivering and quiet. Between them they keeled the horse over onto the ground and the forester sat on its neck while Edwin pulled some hairs from its tail, ran them over a lump of beeswax he held in his hand; and with his bone needle and the waxed hair, drew together the gaping edges of the wound. The animal shuddered when the needle went in, but did not resist. Then Edwin put honey on the

[53]

wound and dressed it with leaves, and cool black mud over all, and then bound it with strips torn from his coarse shirt.

" 'Leave the horse here if you will,' Edwin said to King William, 'and I will send it to you when he is recovered.'

"So Edwin healed the King's horse, and for his sake William spared the village, and let its people keep their rights of grazing and gathering, and for Edwin himself he sent two fine shirts, one of which the Beemaster wore on his wedding day, and one of which he wore to his grave."

Six

The following weekend, Jenny Barnes brought someone to see Cathy.

"This is my friend, Eileen Johnson. The expert I told you about. She knows all about horses."

There was a burst of protesting laughter from the woman Miss Barnes had brought with her.

"No one knows all about horses. I might be some help though, and I've quite a few contacts around here. The ponies I keep wouldn't be any good for what you want. They're Welsh Mountain ponies, only about this high." She sketched a measurement in the air, on a level with her chest. "From what Jenny's told me, you need something bigger: a Forester, perhaps, or something of that type."

"I've asked Dr. Wainwright, Cathy," Jenny Barnes said. "He says it's an excellent idea for Mark to ride so long as there's plenty of help to keep him safe on the pony, and as long as you don't overdo it. He's made us a list of do's and don't's, and given us his blessing. Now all you need is the animal."

Joe Marshall had heard of one or two ponies worth considering, and Mrs. Johnson had some in mind as well, so they decided to spend the day in search. It would be a beginning.

They left Jenny Barnes behind, to keep Mark occupied, and to answer any awkward questions about where Cathy was on such a fine Saturday. Then they set off for Eileen Johnson's house, to transfer to her Land Rover, which would be the best vehicle to use.

"People with horses for sale always seem to live at the furthermost end of the muddiest possible track," she explained.

They drove some miles through the forest, and approached the stud through beechwoods that would soon begin to show green. The trees stood, tall and gray against the brightness of the sky, their feet in last year's leaves. Beyond the trees were close-cropped, banky fields, where little ponies grazed in gangs of three or four, long maned, long tailed, their sides rounded with their coming foals.

"You must come again in May when all the babies are frisking about," Mrs. Johnson said. "They're the prettiest sight ever."

Joe Marshall and Cathy waited in the house while Mrs. Johnson collected some food for a picnic. In the excitement, plans for food hadn't occurred to Cathy. Her mum had been out shopping and they'd left a note for her, otherwise she would have had one organized straight away. To her mind, any outing, however short, needed provision against hunger. If she'd been in charge, her husband had once teased her, they'd never have run out of food at Mafeking.

They waited in a very handsome room, whose only concession to horses was a painting of a stallion, bright gold, with silver-white mane and tail, standing with his head to the wind against a gray Welsh landscape of slate-scarred hills and tumbling water-courses and flying rags of cloud. He seemed to look out into unseen distances with his bright, glowing eyes. There were other paintings in the room too; of landscapes, of flowers, and a splendid embroidery of peacocks. There were books everywhere, and a grand piano with its lid akimbo, as if someone had recently been playing it. Mrs. Johnson was obviously not the sort of woman who could only talk in terms of—what was it Mark had said?—"withers and fetlocks." Mrs. Johnson was all right, Cathy felt.

Jenny Barnes was right to call her an expert, though. As they drove toward the first place on their list she told them all about the care and attention a pony would need, and what the expenses would be and what equipment they would have to buy. It all sounded rather alarming, and Cathy looked sideways at her father to see if he was going off the idea, but he was nodding in agreement as if most of these things had occurred to him already.

"There are some costs you can cut," Eileen Johnson was saying. "Good second-hand leather beats new stuff, I think; and you don't have to dress à la Harry Hall as long as you're warm and comfortable. But you have to remember bills like the blacksmith's. That's skilled work. You can't bodge that up yourself or you'll lame your pony and he will be useless."

Their first call was a disaster. The "nice little cob" they had been told to expect was a gaunt, lugubrious creature, who shuffled out of his stable with a resounding, hollow cough, like a heavy smoker on a bad morning. Cathy felt dreadfully sorry for him. He looked like the pictures of Eeyore: cynical of the world and its affections. They drove on again, down the expected muddy

[57]

tracks and pot-holey lanes. They were shown a beautiful pony with nerves like harp strings: a huge hunter; a mare very obviously in foal, and at one place, a placid, friendly fat fellow that Cathy thought was just right, until Mrs. Johnson picked up his feet. They smelled as if something had died in them.

"It's a crying shame," she said. "It'll take a great deal of time and money to make him really fit again."

From place to place they went, disappointed each time.

"Horse language is like real estate agents' language," Joe Marshall said, after their seventh visit. "Buckingham Palace on paper, and Coronation Street when you get there."

"Do you want to leave it now, and try again next weekend?" asked Mrs. Johnson.

"Just one more, please," Cathy begged.

"Let's hope this one isn't too old, too young, too stubborn, too spirited, too delicate, too big, too small, or afflicted with diverse diseases. Let's look at the advertisement again. 'Highland mare, fourteen hands, quiet in every way,' " Mrs. Johnson read.

"In a pig's eye, probably," said Joe Marshall. "Still, I think we've time for one more visit. It's a good job it's only five acres we've got, not fifty, or Cathy would have brought home all the old crocks we've seen today."

That was probably true, Cathy thought. It was funny, really. She had never joined the pony-mad brigade and certainly didn't intend to start now. Yet the more she saw of these large and, for the most part, docile creatures, so dependent for their health and comfort on the whims of their owners, so prepared to bend their strength to the tasks they were set, when sinew for sinew they were so very much the more powerful—the greater the liking for them grew in her, and she began to look forward to the idea of a pony for itself, as well as a means to help Mark.

After a mile or so they came to the livery stables—"Sutton Court," said the address in the advertisement. It was a splendid place, that looked as though it had once been the stable block belonging to a stately home, though there was no big house in sight. The buildings, with their pillared facade and great arched entrance, were emblazoned on the keystone with the coat of arms of the family that had owned it, and seemed to reflect the grandeur of the vanished house.

"This is one of the places I couldn't get through to on the phone," said Mrs. Johnson. "I hope the owner won't mind us just turning up. It's all rather posh, isn't it?"

They walked through the archway, looking for someone to speak to. It was no less magnificent within the courtyard, around which were box stalls with vaulted roofs, paneled walls, superb ironwork and beautifully tiled floors.

A man emerged from one of these boxes and came to greet them. He was Major Elton, the proprietor, he said, and he was not in the least put out that they had not telephoned for an appointment.

"I'm out a good deal, so I often don't hear it, anyway. I can see you're impressed with my Stately Stables." He laughed. "They're all that's left of Sutton Court, you know. The last owner was a bit dotty and he set fire to the big house. I find all this grand architecture a bit embarrassing, really: gives people the impression I must be stinking rich, when really I'm only a sort of caretaker. The National Trust owns the place. A family came yesterday and had a good look around. I thought they wanted to see the mare I'm selling. Then they came up and asked

[59]

"Spot on, without shoes, and she's eight years old. She's proved barren so far, but you never know, she might spring a surprise one day."

They saddled Moirag then, and Mrs. Johnson rode her out into the paddock. Cathy watched, but she did not speak a word.

Later on, when they had had tea and had visited the pony again to have a further look, she patted the smooth hide, twisted her fingers in the dark mane, and offered pieces of leftover biscuit to the searching, velvet lips that took the scraps from her hand so deftly. Excitement, hope, and an awful fear of disappointment filled Cathy to bursting point and made her chest ache.

"I really think she's the pony you need," Major Elton said. "She'll do practically anything you ask, under saddle or in harness, and she's one hundred percent sound. What's more, she's the kindest creature I've ever known, and so smooth you'd think you were sitting on a cloud. I've never known her to buck; indeed, Highland ponies rarely do; and she'll go willingly all day, do well on any old grazing, and live out in all weathers if need be. The only trouble is, so far we haven't spoken about price, and I am afraid it is very high. She is a registered mare, you see, and in fact she would cost more if she were not barren. I can't offer to negotiate with you either, I'm afraid, for it's the owner who sets the price, and I take my commission on what's paid."

He named the amount, and they knew it was an impossible one. Even calling on all available help, there was no chance at all they could afford to buy Moirag at that price, and the disappointment that each of them felt was reflected on the faces of the others in the little group. It was a very quiet journey home.

didn't have to take it out on her—especially when she was trying so hard to help. But then he wasn't to know. So far it was a secret from him, so it was pretty unreasonable to resent his rudeness, particularly as he was obviously feeling so rotten. She had resented it though; even now, inside herself, were the remaining shadows of "why should it be me who has to be involved with this?" She was surprised at herself, having thought they had all vanished away.

"I'm sorry, Katy-Cat," he said, after a while. "When these stupid limbs get worse, I start feeling they'll be sorry when I'm dead, and all that nonsense, and before long I'm on a downward spiral and taking everyone else with me. Did you see Mother? She looks like the end of the world, and I know darned well it's because I'm so mopey, but I can't cheer up, however hard I try. If I read, my head reels, and my mind's so clogged up with myself that I can't get on with my stories. Tell me not to be such a fool, Cathy. Get angry, or throw something. Tell me to go to hell."

Cathy's own shadows began to melt.

"I don't need to tell you to go," she said. "You look to me to be there already."

He gave himself a shake, like a dog ridding itself of water drops. "Let's go out in the garden," he said. "You'll have to push."

When they were out on the flagged path, he turned his head toward her.

"Is your mother subject to fits?" he said.

"What on earth do you mean?"

"Well, just look at her. She's in your doorway, jumping up and down, and waving her arms. There's something in her hand."

Cathy stared across at her mother, who was now

calling out, but the words were inaudible.

"It's the phone she's holding, you idiot. Someone wants to speak to me. OK if I leave you here?"

"I shan't run away," he said.

"I'll be back. 'Bye for now."

Cathy pelted across the lawn and arrived breathless at the door. Her mother put the phone in her hand.

"It's Major Elton. You'll have to speak to him. Dad's at the pub."

"Hello?" Cathy enquired into the mouthpiece. Her heart was racing. She clutched the phone and listened intently.

"I've some news about the pony," Major Elton said. "I hear your father's out, but I'm sure you'll do just as well. It's about Moirag.

"I spoke to the owner, Mrs. Harris, about your interest in the pony, and I also told her—I hope you don't mind—your reason for wanting Moirag in particular. I knew she would be interested: you'll see in a moment why that's important. She has a daughter, Fiona, a little younger than you, I should think, who had an accident a while ago, and lost the use of her left hand. She used to ride a great deal, and Moirag was bought for her to use, but now she won't ride, has few friends, and she's a bit of a problem. Mrs. Harris is prepared to drop the price for Moirag, if you will try to help Fiona a little: try to bring her out of herself."

The shadows came flooding back. Why me again, Cathy thought. How can I guarantee to make friends with a girl I've never met, and even if she's the best thing since sliced bread, why can't I be allowed to have nice, uncomplicated, ordinary friends with no problems? It's not fair. Really it isn't.

Then she remembered Moirag, and the deerlike

gentleness of her face, and the delicate, seeking muzzle. Once Moirag was at Beamsters, if Fiona chose not to be friends, Moirag could hardly be taken back, could she? Anyway, anything was worth trying, if it meant they could have Moirag.

"Are you there, Cathy?"

"Sorry, Major Elton, I was just thinking. If Mrs. Harris thinks it will work, I'll do my best. Shall I ask Dad to ring you back?"

"That's the best thing. Then I can tell him the new price and see what he says."

Even with the concession, it was a lot of money: more than Joe Marshall had reckoned on spending, but if Cathy was prepared to take on the job of Fiona Harris—and privately he thought it might well be a rotten one—then he was prepared to stretch his resources a little. It would be worth it for such an animal. She was a real cracker, and just exactly right. He couldn't wait to see Mark's face.

Major Elton arranged that Mrs. Harris should come over the next evening to settle the matter, and that, all being well, Moirag would be sent over later in the week.

Jean Marshall was glad to see her family in something like its right mind again.

"You can smarten yourselves up now," she said. "Church, this evening. I'm not having us turning into a Weddings, Funerals and Harvest Festivals lot."

"Oh, Mum," Cathy protested. "I can't stand that vicar chap. He sounds as though he's being strangled."

"It won't be him anymore. He's only been standing

in for our proper rector, apparently, who's just come back from abroad. Quite handsome, I believe."

"Come on then, Cathy. We can't miss the chance of a handsome vicar, can we?" Joe Marshall laughed.

"Rector," his wife said, refusing to rise to his bait. "Just you hurry up and get ready."

Saint Michael's was a very old church, with a saddle-back Saxon tower and massive round Norman arches. Cathy wondered if Mark's first Beemaster had worshipped there. He would not have seen that monstrous Victorian window glass though, nor all those marble monuments to innumerable generations of a family called Passingham. Three of them lay in effigy in a side aisle, looking for all the world as though they were enjoying an everlasting tea party, for only one of them was entirely recumbent, and of the other two, the man was propped up on one elbow, while the woman knelt with one hand outstretched, presumably toward heaven but it did seem exactly as though she were offering her companions a sandwich.

Cathy giggled quietly to herself, and Mr. Marshall looked fiercely at her, but then he saw the effigies and smothered a grin.

The hymns and prayers were soon over, and John Burton, the rector, who believed in short sermons, released his congregation into the air again. He put a hand on Cathy's arm as she came into the porch, though, and said how pleased he was to see them all.

"I saw how interested you were in our statuary," he remarked to Cathy.

She was not sure how to reply to this remark.

"They're terrible, aren't they?" he went on cheerfully. "I call them The Three Bears. If you can spare the time I can show you some far more interesting monuments."

[66]

"Thank you," Mrs. Marshall said. "Have you any brasses?"

"Yes; it's those I'd like to show you. There are some earlier Passinghams of course; we can't seem to escape from them. They remind me of my favorite curate story, about the nervous young fellow who was conducting a service in a church in the north, where most of the Percy family was commemorated—you remember the legends of the Percys and the Douglasses? Well, it seems there were family tablets and urns and effigies all over the place, and the poor young man launched into prayer with 'Almighty and most Perciful Father'!

"Here are Richard and Margaret Passingham in this seventeenth-century brass, with their sixteen children, and a very fulsome bit of Latin around the edge saying how virtuous they all were. I wonder what they were really like. There's a very splendid knight on the floor of the Lady Chapel who wasn't a Passingham, but he married one. He's been rubbed so many times, poor chap, that he's beginning to wear away, and I've had to limit the number of rubbings people make. This is the memorial I thought you would find most interesting, though."

He showed them a dark tablet set in the wall near the pulpit, looking at least as old as many of the other brasses, but its inscription was in English rather than in Latin. The oddly spelled words were cramped together in gothic script, though, and Mr. Burton had to read it out for them.

"Sacred to the memory of Robert Lydyard, born in London in the year of our Lord 1640 and died in this parish on the 14th day of May 1698,

[67]

who in 1665 was cured by miracle of the Plague, and God be thanked no man else here suffered the disease."

"Golly," Cathy said. "Mark would be interested in that."

"Mark Anderson, do you mean? Goodness, he's had every scrap of information he could squeeze out of me about our friend Lydyard. You see there is a strong connection between this memorial and your house. The woman who is said to have cured him apparently lived at Beamsters, and if you know of Mark's interest in the house you'll realize how eagerly he seized on that information."

"I certainly do," laughed Cathy. "I'll get him to tell me all about it."

"So you've made friends with him, have you? I'm glad to hear it. He can be a bit of a porcupine, but he's a bright boy, and well worth winning over. Tell him I'm coming across to see him soon, will you, to bring him some papers he wanted, and to tell him all about my adventures abroad."

"Yes, I will," Cathy said.

They all walked home in the dusk, and Cathy was really glad it was the old black-and-white house they were going back to, this old, settled place that held within itself the essence of people now dead and gone, and yet somehow still part of the fabric. As she had reasoned before, you could not say it was haunted, or possessed, for that seemed to imply unhappy spirits, held unwilling prisoner, yet any of the people Mark had described to her could have appeared to Cathy within the walls of Beamsters without causing her the least shock of amazement, so vividly had he portrayed them for her, and so much part of the place were they.

Mark's mother brought him over that evening to see if his Scrabble board was ready. He was a real fanatic of the game, and Mr. Marshall had offered to make him a special board with large wooden letter blocks which were easier than the usual-sized plastic ones for his unpredictable hands to cope with.

The game was ready, so he and Cathy sat down to play. He was very slow at first. Her fingers itched to help him. She sat on her hands till it was her turn.

"I heard you writing this afternoon," Cathy said, putting her first word down.

"You're nuts," Mark replied. "You can't hear people writing, unless they're using squeaky chalk or one of those quill things that makes a scratching noise."

He prefixed the word she had made with "un" and she glowered at him. "Well, talking into the recorder then. I heard you when I was in the garden. Your window was open," she said. " 'Telling a Story' sounds like something out of Listen with Mother. Perhaps one ought to use the 'playwright' spelling for 'wrighting' like that."

"I like that," Mark said. "Gives it a sort of dignity, like a craft. Weaving the threads of the story together like the old minstrels who sang to the harp."

" 'Spinning a yarn,' " said Cathy, putting down her next word.

" 'Losing the thread.' "

" 'Cottoning on!' Now we've hurtled from the Celtic mists to the dark satanic mills in five seconds flat."

"True," said Mark. "But as for you, you'll never weave spells if you can't spell 'weave.' You've put it with two e's."

[69]

"Oh no, I haven't spelled it wrong!" Cathy added a triumphant L to the word she had made.

"It's 'weevil,' not 'weevel,' " argued Mark.

"And what's the difference between a boll weevil and the biscuit weevil?" asked Cathy.

"What, for goodness sake? I give up."

"The biscuit weevil is the lesser of the two weevils," Cathy giggled.

That broke up the game altogether, and they began instead to pelt each other with absurd jokes, forgetting the time so completely that Mrs. Anderson had to come over and remind Mark it was time for bed.

She was so pleased to see him looking happy; but her delight seemed to sour his mood, and he snapped at her. "What have you come for? Were you afraid I'd run away?"

Mrs. Anderson smiled and made no remark, but Cathy saw the brightness fade out of her face. All she said was "Come over when you're ready then. I'll go and put the kettle on for your hot water bottle."

"Why are you so rotten to your mother?" Cathy asked when Mrs. Anderson had left.

"Because she gave me this damned disease, that's why," Mark said. "Women carry it, you know."

"It's not her fault, surely?"

"Of course it isn't. I know that. But I know she feels guilty about it, and something makes me bait her, which only makes it worse. It's like wanting to prod an aching tooth. You know it'll hurt but you can't help doing it. I wish she didn't care a hoot about me. I don't want to be like this about her. What can I do, Cath?"

Cathy thought hard. She wanted to say the unkindest thing she could think of so that it would act as a cautery, somehow, and clean the poison out of him. Whether it would work or not she did not know. She wished she were older, cleverer. How could she help someone like him when sometimes she found herself quite difficult enough.

Her voice came out cold and nasty. "She could have put you in a home, you know."

She looked at him, completely coldly, her friendship for him all hidden away. He didn't react with anger, as she'd hoped he might, but slumped even further in his chair. She had failed. That was obvious.

"It might have been better at that," he said. "She only keeps me here because she feels she owes me that much."

Now Cathy herself was angry, with no pretense in it.

"That's not true," she flared at him. "And you know it!"

"It's not true," Mark repeated. "And I know it. Smile at me, Katy-Cat. At least I know when I'm being a louse."

"All right then," she relented. It would all be so much easier if she didn't like him.

"And you'll listen to the next part of my story?"

"Yes, I will. That reminds me. Mr. Burton said you could tell me all about Robert Lydyard, and the tablet in the church." That had the right effect. He brightened at once.

"Listen to the tape." Mark said. "You'll hear all about him. There's a lot on this tape though, so leave yourself plenty of time."

Later, when she was in bed, Cathy settled herself down with pillows behind her and Thred Bear in the crook of her arm, and switched the recorder to replay. Mark's voice began to speak, telling her more of the story of

[71]

Beamsters. He spoke of times when the land around it lay waste, and no one dared go abroad in the forest for fear of what he might find, or what might happen to him. He spoke of King John and his love for the forest; a bad man, perhaps, but a good deal better at being King than people gave him credit for. He told how slow change came to the forest with time, though not the upheavals of enclosure and dispossession that so much of the land knew, for this was not sheep country, and the forest would not produce coin for the fleece-lined pockets of the merchants. Indeed, even the major events that ebbed and flowed around Beamsters, struggles for power, foreign wars, attempted invasions, scarcely touched its serenity, till old Will Saywell's two sons set each to a different cause in the Civil War, and both were killed in it. Will had been Beemaster for many years, and it was understood that one of his sons should take his place eventually. The whole village grieved for him, and did what they could, but it was the death of the old man. That left only his daughter Sarah. As a child she had seen her mother burned as a witch by King James' men, and she had been strange ever since. Her old cousin Tobit came to live with her for a while until he too died, and she was left alone at Beamsters with only the bees for company and the herb garden for her comfort, and so she lived for many years.

Now the tape arrived at the part of the story Cathy had been wondering about.

"The old woman had lit a fire under a great tub of water outside the house, and was piling sheets and clothing on the grass nearby. She had herbs in her hand that she had picked from the garden, and these she threw

[72]

into the water as it began to steam. It was a bright, beautiful day, and the sunlight made the shadows of the encircling forest darker than ever. The tang of the smoke was sharp in the air. The woman worked cheerfully, smiling and singing to herself in the way of one who is alone for the most part, and content to be so.

"Something was coming out of the forest toward her; a huddled, hurrying figure; hurrying, that is, as much as complete exhaustion would allow. There was little noise to the progress, but old Sarah was aware of it, and turned to peer into the gloom; looking, in her coarse brown dress, like an old shaggy bear, shortsighted and suspicious.

"Whatever it was that limped and halted had scarcely got itself out of the shadow of the trees when it fell in a heap in the path and lay still.

"Sarah walked over to it, cautiously, and poked at it with her stick. Then, stooping, she pulled back the tattered cloak it wore to reveal the figure of a man, quite young, pitifully thin, and with his shoes worn through to the soles of his feet. She swiftly appraised his condition, dreadful enough in itself, but more horrifying still when she saw the marks on his face.

" 'So,' she muttered. 'Where do you come from, I wonder, bringing us such a gift, and one we could well do without?' She prodded the unconscious figure more vigorously with her stick.

" 'Get up!' she said. 'Get up quickly. Lie there with the rosy death on you and you'll be in your grave by sunset.'

"The man roused himself and struggled to his feet, babbling nonsensically, and shaking with fever and fear. 'Dead. All dead . . . all gone. Don't shut me in! The cart—

the cart—to the pit—I will not go to the pit. Here's a fine rat—rat—rats in the pit. Let me out, let me out, let me out!'

" 'Be quiet!' the old woman snapped at him, and he collected himself for a moment, saw her fierce face and recoiled from her. Her expression softened at the sight of his exhausted, frightened eyes.

" 'You need have no fear of an old woman. Come with me and I will help you, but you must do all that I say. First, strip yourself of your clothes. Yes, all of them!'

"She turned to the fire and pulled the iron tub away, testing the heat of the water, which seemed to satisfy her. Then with her stick she took the rags he had discarded and threw them on the fire, before pushing the shuddering traveler into the tub, where she washed him gently, as if he were a tiny child. She gathered from among his ravings that his name was Robert Lydyard, that he had come from London where he had escaped from a house shut up in the Plague, where his wife and babies now lay dead. He had stolen a horse and started to travel and had ridden fast for several days as if they might catch him and take him back to that fearful house. Then the horse had gone lame and he had turned it away and begun to walk. He had no idea how long he had been walking. He began to struggle then as she soaped his head and poured water over him.

" 'Think me mad if you will, Robert Lydyard,' she chided him. 'People mostly do. But unless you do as I wish I'll not stir a hand to help you.'

"Then she hauled him out, chattering and shivering and brought him a clean robe of scarlet wool, with bunches of herbs sewn to it here and there; sweet herbs and rank dog-garlic. Next, she took him to the bee-skeps and made him kneel down, and she spoke to the bees who were buzzing angrily as they sensed a stranger.

" 'He has the Plague, this man. He will die, or he will not die, according to God's will.'

"She gave them these words as a statement, not asking anything of them. Her asking she kept for the Creator Himself, and she prayed now, rapidly and forcefully, as if she dared the powers of Heaven not to listen, and lastly she laid her hands on the young man's head, and recited over him:

" 'I will say unto the Lord, Thou art my hope and my stronghold: My God, in him will I trust.

For he shall deliver thee from the snare of the hunter: and from the noisome pestilence.

He shall defend thee under his wings, and thou shall be safe under his feathers.

His faithfulness and trust shall be thy shield and buckler.

Thou shalt not be afraid for any terror by night; nor for the arrow that flieth by day.

For the pestilence that walketh in darkness; nor for the sickness that destroyeth in the noonday.

A thousand shall fall beside thee, and ten thousand at thy right hand, but it shall not come nigh thee.' "

"Then she took the young man into her house and put him into a bed near the wall. There was no speck of dirt anywhere in the house.

"Each day she washed the clothing from his bed, and renewed the herbs in his woollen robe. She gathered

[75]

them from her own garden, from her storehouse, and from the forest around: devil's bit, fleabane, germander, wood sorrel and starwort. Some she made salves from, some she infused to make herb tea with honey in it, for his mouth and throat were sore and swollen. She watched over him constantly until at last the boils on his face and body gathered and burst, and there was no trace of blackness in the wounds. She knew then that there was a good chance for him. After that, she chased him out daily and washed him in the tub, and dressed his sores with honey. He thought her quite mad. He had never been washed so much in all his life. But he was getting better, and the foul disease that had killed his family and half the city had left him, thin, gray and exhausted, but blessedly alive, thanks to God's providence in the shape of this amazing woman.

" 'Is there magic in this old tub of yours,' he asked her, 'that you chase me into it each day like a new baptism?'

" 'No magic but what is in God's good water everywhere,' she chided him, 'and in the creatures and plants He gives us for healing. You should thank Him yourself, and tell the bees you have done so, for all matters of importance should be told them.'

"So he went, feeling rather foolish, and told the bees that he had recovered, and they murmured in their skeps, but without anger, for now he was no stranger. And as he stood there and saw all around him the beauty of the forest, he realized that he could never leave it; and why should he, for his old life had died with his family and friends. So, when his strengths had come back, and he guessed that the chaos the Plague had brought on his old home would be past, he sent for such money and possessions as he had, and found a house and land not far from Beamsters. Then, while she lived no one dare say or do anything that might offend Sarah Saywell in his presence; and when she died, it was Robert Lydyard who told the bees, and saw to her burial in the churchyard; planting young lime trees near her grave, and sweetsmelling flowers upon it, so that her old dear friends should visit her all summer long."

The tape clicked, and for a moment the recorder went on humming around, until Cathy roused herself from Mark's dream of the past, and switched off the machine and fell asleep.

Eight

Nothing could possibly have horrified Cathy more than her first sight of Mrs. Harris. Her face was long, and her mouth was all teeth, and her sawlike voice said "hice" for "house," and her head scarf and trews and quilted jacket were the uniform of all that Mark had declared he could not abide.

"I'm awfully glad you're having our pony," she announced when she came to see the Marshalls. "I'm sure she'll do splendidly for a disabled rider. If you want her grooming kit, tack and stuff like that, let me know and I'll bring it across. I'll bring Fiona with me when we transport the pony. She wouldn't come today: she's out somewhere with the dogs." The strident voice announced this as if they were all slightly deaf.

Jean Marshall enquired about Fiona's accident.

"She had a fall," Mrs. Harris said. "She's ridden since she was tiny, on her little Dartmoor pony, Dusky, but Dusky's too small now and I'd bought Moirag as a birthday present and left her at Sutton Court, to be a surprise you see, for the great day. Then Fiona went out riding about a week before her birthday, with a friend she was staying with, on a couple of young horses that they really weren't supposed to take out at all. Fiona had a crashing fall over a low fence and the friend's horse landed close by and crushed Fiona's hand. We thought she'd lose the hand altogether, but even as it is, it's virtually useless."

Cathy felt all kinds of feelings churning inside her, but over all a sense of shame, knowing she should be sorry for this woman and her unfortunate daughter, when all she could really concentrate on was how much Mark was bound to dislike her. And if Fiona were of the same stamp, it would be all quite impossible.

"Ever since she came out of hospital she's wanted to hide herself away," Mrs. Harris continued. "She won't go near Dusky, let alone consider a new pony. She has to go for exercises, but they say she makes no effort at all. It's really most disheartening. I tell her there are others far worse off, but she won't listen. All her friends ride, of course, but they're off every weekend competing and haven't got time for a crock like Fiona."

Here the voice quietened a little. "She's lost everything she used to enjoy, and when I heard that you were hoping to teach your crippled neighbor to ride, I just wondered if you might be the person to help Fiona too."

"Mark doesn't even know about the riding, yet," Cathy replied. "It's a secret, so far. Give me a chance to get him used to the idea first, will you, before Fiona comes?"

What she really meant was to let Mark get really keen on riding, and fond of Moirag, before he found the fly in the ointment.

"Of course," Mrs. Harris replied, "I do understand. I won't bring Fiona when I drive the truck over then. She can come across in a week or so, when everything's under way."

[79]

When Mrs. Harris rose to leave, Cathy went with her to the door.

"By the way, I ought to apologize, I suppose," Mrs. Harris said, "for calling Mark a cripple. They ticked me off good and proper at the hospital for using that term."

"That's all right," Cathy said. "It is a depressing word, though, isn't it?"

The horsey face smiled. "You're right." Then, after a moment's consideration, "I'm allowed 'handicapped,' am I? It doesn't sound so permanent, does it? After all, handicaps can be overcome, can't they, like in golf and horse racing and so on?"

Mrs. Harris was trying so hard to get it right that Cathy felt almost sorry for her, and a small liking for the woman grew in Cathy, despite her daunting appearance and cut-glass voice. And, anyway, she was going to sell them Moirag.

Spring would soon merge into summer. Even the oaks were shyly admitting the first glimmer of their new green. The Beamsters garden sprang surprises each day, with new flowers, new growth that the Marshalls had not discovered or suspected. The vegetables thrust up their first leaves in the vegetable garden, and the broad beans, bravest of all, were almost ready for their stakes. Cathy had inspected them, and was just pulling out a few spindly weeds, when she heard the sound of an engine, and saw a heavy vehicle approaching. She knew at once what it was, and her heart began to thump and her hands to tingle. In preparation for this moment, she and her father had cleared and cleaned and creosoted the old stable, put broom and pitchfork and wheelbarrow all ready, marked buckets with white-painted letters, and checked the feed store for someting suitable for ponies.

"She won't want dairy rations or pignuts or layers' mash, that's for sure," Joe Marshall had said.

The largest piece of equipment had arrived the previous day. Miss Barnes had turned up, quite amazingly, with a tractor and trailer belonging to a neighbor of hers who ran a nursery garden next to some civic buildings that were being demolished. One of the items thrown out to be burned was a conductor's rostrum, which she had purchased for a pound or so, and brought with her on the trailer.

"Put a ramp down one side, paint it up a bit, and there's your wheelchair mounting block," she announced, delighted with her find. Joe Marshall thought she'd been really very clever.

"I can fix it easily," he said.

Now Moirag was arriving, and Cathy could see Mrs. Marshall coming out of the house. She must have heard the rumble of the engine. At the same time Joe Marshall emerged from the barn.

"The pony's come," Cathy shouted.

"How do you know?" asked her mother. "It could be cows."

"I haven't ordered any cows," laughed Joe Marshall, "and anyway, who'd send cows in a posh trailer like that? This year's model, too. Look at the license plate."

The trailer drew up in the yard, and Mrs. Harris got down from the cab to let down the tailgate. Moirag looked at them out of the dark interior of the trailer, and then walked down the ramp to them, looking about her with curiosity.

"Where would you like her?" Mrs. Harris asked, and

[81]

Cathy led the way to the stable. Moirag walked in with supreme lack of concern and began to eat the feed in the manger.

"I'll show you the field, too," Cathy offered. She was proud of their field, with its railed fence and stout gate, and the sleek cattle that grazed in it.

"Splendid. Splendid," said Mrs. Harris.

When she had driven the horse trailer away, the Marshalls went to look more closely at Moirag.

"Isn't she a love?" said Cathy's mum. "And what a nice color: like toast."

"It's called dun," Cathy told her. "She's really gentle, Mum. Just feel her soft nose."

Later, Cathy sat on Moirag, just for a moment, just to see what it felt like. It was very strange, and not at all similar to a bicycle that is being imagined into a horse. She felt she might grow to enjoy it though.

Waiting to show her to Mark was unbearable. It had to be casual, off-the-cuff, throwaway. "Oh, by the way Mark, we've got a pony. Would you like to see it?"

It was Joe Marshall who just happened to be leading Moirag across the lawn on a piece of rope as Margaret Anderson just happened to be wheeling Mark out of the house for an airing.

"Hello, Mark," he said. "What do you think of my petrol-saving device?"

Expressions flickered across Mark's face so quickly that they were impossible to interpret singly, but there was something like longing in his eye, and a hint of suspicion, and possibly a gleam of determination too.

[82]

"Very nice," he said.

"Cathy sat on her this morning," Joe went on. "Looks a treat up there, our Cath does."

"I bet."

"Fancy a ride sometime?" He had not meant to suggest it so soon. His enthusiasm for the whole project had got the better of him, and he knew he could have said just the wrong thing. It implied that he knew already about Mark's longing to ride, which had been a confidence to Cathy. It might make the whole plot too obvious.

"I wouldn't mind," Mark said carefully, but his hands gripped the chair handles as hard as they were able.

"After tea, then. OK? Miss Barnes is coming, isn't she? She might lend a hand, perhaps."

On the dot of five, Miss Barnes arrived, and Eileen Johnson came too, summoned by the grapevine to Mark's first real encounter with Moirag. It was as well she came, for without her they all felt they would never have resolved the pile of straps and buckles and oddments of leather with which the pony had to be clothed before it could be ridden.

"I've brought a hat, too. He must always wear one, even if he is going at a snail's pace. I hope it fits!"

"They made him wear one at Chalgrove Hall. I think he felt a bit of an idiot in it," said Cathy.

"He'd be more of an idiot without it, if he fell on his head," Jenny Barnes remarked. "Right. We seem to be ready. I'll bring Mark across."

While she was gone, Joe Marshall checked the rostrum, anxious that it should do its job and not let his workmanship down. "The nails are still hot in it," he said. He had positioned it facing a railed fence, so that there was a gap about a meter wide between the fence and the rostrum, so that Moirag would be contained in a sort of corridor, and unable to swing away as they maneuvered Mark aboard.

He was coming toward them now, still looking carefully casual.

"What's that?" he called out. "A launching pad?"

"You could call it that!" Joe Marshall said. "It's to help me load sacks, without breaking my back," he added hastily. After all he *could* use the platform for just that purpose. "Come on, Apollo 18, let's get you ready for liftoff."

They pushed the wheelchair up the ramp, put on the brake, and blocked the wheels with bricks so that the chair could not shift. Cathy brought Moirag alongside, and spoke softly to her while the others, directed by Jenny Barnes, heaved Mark on to the pony's back. It looked an uncomfortable procedure for him, but he made no complaint, except a half-amused one when Eileen Johnson set the hat on his head. Mrs. Johnson fetched some hay from the stable and padded it a bit. "I'll bring a smaller size," she said, "for next time."

Cathy looked up at him sitting so high, his hands hooked through the broad leather strap they had buckled about the pony's neck.

"Are you ready?" she said.

He nodded. He looked at her, and there was something in his expression that was a secret message, just for her, that said, "I know you did this for me: I shall never tell you in words that I know, because it would spoil things."

Cathy led the pony, and with Miss Barnes and Mrs. Johnson supporting him, Mark began his first ride on Moirag, who stepped as gently as if she knew her rider's disabilities, her pace even, her head nodding to her own

[84]

rhythm, hoofs muffled by the softness of the turf on which she walked.

He sat so well on her that the two women stepped back; at hand, but not holding him, and he rode with his head up, proud as an eagle on a mountain. Jean Marshall, watching from the kitchen doorway, saw that from the window of Lawn End Mrs. Anderson was watching too.

They made no effort to teach him, that first session, but just led him about and let him enjoy the freedom that he had so longed for. His supreme pleasure was infectious: they spent far more time than they had intended. At last, though, Jenny Barnes said, "Enough for today, I think, Mark."

"OK, Andy Pandy, back in your box," Mark said, but there was no bitterness in it. They got him into his chair, and Moirag put her nose into his lap and huffed at him, her breath warm and sweet.

"Hello, you old haybag," he said, gently caressing her nose, scratching her neck under the blue-black mane. "Thanks for the ride."

Cathy pushed him back to the house, where his mother was waiting. She longed to ask him, to assure herself, if he really, *really* enjoyed it, as much as it appeared he had; whether it measured up to his dreams. But she stopped herself. She knew it wouldn't do. He would tell her in his own time.

"Hey, I've been riding," he announced to his mother.

"I saw," she said. "Was it fun?"

"Not bad," he said, and asked Cathy to take him to his room, where he kept his tapes.

"Can I give you some more stuff to listen to, Cathy?" he asked. "I've been revising what I've done: changing some of the words, putting more information in. It wasn't all just as I wanted it. Would you listen and see if it's any better? I've got a little more to do, and then I could ask Mum to bring it over."

"OK," Cathy said. "I liked the story of Sarah Saywell, by the way. Is it all true?"

"True, with a bit of imagination added. What it says on the tablet is certainly true, and there are still lime trees in the churchyard, though the old woman's grave has disappeared. It could be any of those green bumps under the wall. And she really did cure Lydyard of the Plague."

"It was fleas, wasn't it?"

"That carried the Plague, you mean? Yes, rat fleas. I don't know whether old Sarah knew that, but I don't think any flea could have survived her passion for cleanliness. The ones she didn't burn she must have drowned. No wonder everyone thought her so odd. Washing wasn't much in fashion in those days. Still, getting rid of the fleas wouldn't help someone who already got the disease, so there must have been something in the herbs and honey that cured him."

"Either that, or he didn't dare die with old Sarah bustling him about," Cathy said.

"You'd have to ask the bees about that!" Mark laughed. "Still, she may have had some knowledge out of her time, like Leonardo and his airplane, or H. G. Wells and the rocket, or more likely it was some old country kill-or-cure that just happened to work."

"I'd ask the bees, if I could," said Cathy. "I wonder why there are no bees at Beamsters now? There's no sign that bees were ever kept here, and all the bees in the garden are just passing through. They look a bit busy for a chat!"

"It does seem odd," Mark replied. "Your great-uncle tried very hard to get them established, when I'd told him about the history of the place. He bought hives and skeps and smokers, and all the gear, and took as much expert advice as he could get hold of, but it just didn't work. I don't know whether it was bad luck, or whether he was a rotten apiarist, but he had one disaster after another. He had mice on some of his hives one winter, and then badgers came into the garden and knocked over some of the others. Finally the ones he had left were struck with foul brood, and so he gave up, and burned his hives and never tried again. It seemed such a shame, because he'd planted all sorts of stuff in the garden to attract them and keep them well supplied. It just seems as though the place doesn't want the bees anymore."

"Perhaps they'll come back," said Cathy. "Though I'm not entirely sure I'd want them to. I've always been a bit afraid of them."

"You should read up about them. They're very interesting, you know."

"All right, I'll do that. I must go back now and help with supper or I'll be in the doghouse. Send the tapes over when you're ready. I'll listen."

That night, in the listening quiet of the old house, Cathy replayed the Beamsters tapes, hearing Mark's revisions: he had added new material, altered sentences here and there, changed a word to one that seemed to sharpen the meaning. It really was a craft, this word-business, Cathy decided; like choosing colors for embroidery, or finding the right grain of the wood. She listened again to the story of Sarah Saywell and the young man with the Plague until the tape spun out the last sentence. She was about to switch it off, when, unexpectedly, Mark's voice spoke again.

"I've been looking through some books of my father's. I found these two lines of verse: they're off a tombstone, but I don't suppose that matters. They're for you, from me, because of this afternoon.

> Betwixt the stirrup and the ground,
> Mercy I asked: mercy I found.

Good night, Katy-Cat. God bless. See you tomorrow."

Nine

To add respectability to the fiction that Moirag had been bought to help Joe Marshall with his work, he used her to carry sacks of feed from the barn to the customers' cars. She didn't mind the work in the least. Then Mr. Roberts from the farm found a set of workable harness and an old flat bed cart, so battered that he had never thought of selling it, but still serviceable. The pony took this, too, in her kindly and equable stride. She was plainly to be seen, doing her work, and not for another few days was Mark offered his second ride. Cathy, nearly exploding with impatience to offer it, seeing how much it meant to him, and knowing he would never ask, was irked by her father's deliberate holding back. The fact that underneath she knew he was right, didn't help her impatience in the least, but Joe Marshall just grinned at the faces she pulled, and went his own way.

"We've got to wait and see Jenny Barnes first anyway," he said, "or we may end up doing him more harm than good."

"When can she come?" said Cathy, pouncing.

"Cathy, I don't know. We must wait. She's busy at the hospital."

As it turned out, the afternoon of her next visit was ideal for riding. Everyone was about, to help if they were needed, the sun was strong and warm, burnishing Moirag's beautiful coat, so she looked like part of the sunlight herself, and Mark was in a mood to match the weather. When they had wheeled him up on to the rostrum, he blew a raucous fanfare on an imaginary trumpet.

"Tara-tara-tar: Lay-dees an gennelmen. Roll hup for the greatest show on earth. See the world's finest heequestrian feats performed before your very eyes."

Jenny Barnes had been working out the easiest way to get Mark aboard. He had some strength in his left leg, and by pushing on this he could help to put his behind in the saddle. Then she lifted his right leg over the pony's neck and lowered it down to place his right foot gently in the stirrup.

"Eileen says we're to work out a compromise between what's 'correct' and what Mark can do. He's got to be comfortable and secure, and not put too much strain on the weaker parts of himself. She's sent this, by the way."

Miss Barnes showed them a wide leather belt with handles on it. "It's for Mark, not Moirag," she explained.

"They had those at Chalgrove," Mark said. "Ycu all grab hold if I start to fall off." He helped them buckle the belt around his waist, and patted the gleaming leather approvingly.

"My goodness, don't I look the thing. Every inch a hofficer and a gentleman."

They took him about the field, and Jenny Barnes gave him exercises to do, which made him laugh so much he nearly fell off, and then he took the reins in his left hand, which was the stronger, and with Cathy close by, rode, just for a moment or so, unheld, unled, concentrating his entire attention on what he was doing: as absorbed by it as Cathy imagined he must be by his word craft. She wanted to thank him for sending her the verse, but thought she had better not. Thanks were such awkward things to put into words, and it was too good an afternoon to spoil.

Then, with dismay, she saw the Harrises' horse trailer approaching the yard, and for a moment, felt an awful apprehension that Mrs. Harris had changed her mind and had come to take Moirag away. That was ridiculous, of course. She was bought and paid for.

Mark saw the truck pull into the yard, saw Mrs. Harris get down from the cab, watched her walking toward them.

"Who's that?" he asked.

"Moirag's owner. I mean, she used to own Moirag," Cathy explained. Perhaps Mrs. Harris would have changed in some way. Perhaps she had not been quite as dyed-in-the-wool horsey as Cathy remembered. Perhaps her voice was not really as bad as all that. . . . But she was just the same: maybe worse, for her face was adorned with a bright and jolly smile.

"I say. She's looking awfully well, isn't she?" Mrs. Harris declared, regarding Moirag. "Enjoying your ride?" She beamed at Mark: all teeth and head scarf.

"Yes, thank you," said Mark, in an excessively polite voice.

"She's a super pony. Give you lots of fun, I'm sure. I've brought Fiona with me, Cathy. Come across and meet her, will you?"

"All right," Cathy said, feeling that "right" was the last thing anything was. "I'll take Mark back to Miss Barnes, and then I'll come over."

"God!" Mark exploded, when Mrs. Harris was scarcely out of earshot. "What a dreadful woman."

Cathy could not think of anything to say. As she led Moirag back toward the gate, Mark began in a whinnying voice that was a cruel caricature of Mrs. Harris':

> "It's awfully bad luck on Diana
> Her ponies have swallowed their bits
> She's fished down their throats with a spanner
> And frightened them all into fits."

"Mark, don't," Cathy pleaded. "She'll hear you."

"Probably," Mark said. "What's she come for, anyway: to make sure your Dad's doing his groom's duties all right? And who's Fiona?"

"Her daughter. She's lonely. I said I'd be friends with her." Cathy's voice was flat with unhappiness.

"Not if she's like her mother, for heaven's sake. Don't touch her with a bargepole."

"Oh, give her a chance," Cathy said, growing angry now. "We haven't even seen her yet. She may be OK. She had an accident and hurt her hand, and she's feeling a bit miserable, that's all. She might be very nice."

"With a mother like that? Some hopes."

In the yard, Mrs. Harris was standing by the open door of the cab of the horse trailer.

"I have to take Dusky over to some little cousins of Fiona's. They may as well use the pony—she's only eating her head off in our paddock. So I thought I'd leave Fiona here for a while if I may. You can get to know each other."

[92]

Sitting like a stone on the high seat, her face registering no expression whatsoever, was a thin, pale girl with a fair braid of hair and eyes the color of the sea in winter.

"Come down, Fiona," her mother said. She came down. She was obviously no more enthusiastic about this enforced "friendship" than were Cathy and Mark. Her damaged hand was pulled up into the sleeve of her coat. The other she put briefly into Cathy's grip and said, "Afternoon," abruptly, and in a voice as soft as her mother's was strident.

The next two hours were like walking through mud. Mark was sulking because of the intrusion into his happiness of the two Harrises, whom, by that evening, he had firmly labeled the Horsey Horror and the Dismal Daughter. Cathy was anxiously trying to draw some response out of the wretched Fiona, whose only wish seemed to be to remain invisible. She drew back from all Cathy's advances of friendship, exactly as she drew back from any contact with Moirag. Of Mark she seemed utterly terrified. She would not even look at him. Cathy felt very low.

Jenny Barnes watched the progress of their relationship, or at least the lack of it, and felt worry for all three of them. She knew from her colleagues the history of Fiona's accident, and knew how little progress anyone had made with her. What magic did Mrs. Harris expect from poor Cathy? As for Mark, she had been sad to see the pleasure leave his face when the Harrises arrived. Well, she would do what she could to help, but she doubted any of them would achieve very much. Perhaps Eileen Johnson might have some ideas.

When Cathy went across to Lawn End after tea, to offer Mark a Scrabble game in compensation, in however small measure, for the destruction of their afternoon, she found him surrounded by papers and feeling a great deal more cheerful.

"Old Burton's brought me over some more notes about Beamsters," he said. "That rectory library's a real treasure house. Oh, and by the way he's sent a couple of articles on beekeeping that I asked him to get for you. Mr. Armitage sent a book on the history of beekeeping too. We were talking about it last week."

"What's he like—Mr. Armitage?" Cathy asked. "Isn't it a bit dull, all by yourself, with one teacher?"

"No. I like it. Armitage is an interesting chap. I just wish he could give me more time, but two hours a day is all I'm allowed. Mind you, they're pretty elastic hours, if we get on the trail of anything interesting."

"Wouldn't you like more company?"

"Not me. I'm choosy about my company." He grinned, remembering the Harrises. "I never was one for all this team spirit, jolly rugger-boot stuff, which is just as well as things are, I suppose, but I honestly don't think I'd have liked that sort of thing much anyway. Mr. Armitage knows his English Lit and helps me when I'm stuck for words, and doesn't think it's the end of the world when I'm feeling bolshie and lead him a dance. He taught me that Horsey Poem—about Diana, what, what! It's John Betjeman, you know, the chap who writes about bronzed, tennis-playing young women, and tries to stop people knocking down Victorian public loos, and so on. Armitage helped him run a campaign to save the Baths at Bucklehurst. You've seen them I expect—that extraordinary building that looks as though it's made out of dirty icing sugar."

"There's no accounting for taste," Cathy said. "They

can knock it down tomorrow as far as I'm concerned."

"Philistine," said Mark. "What if they wanted to knock down Beamsters?"

"Over my dead body." Cathy realized, inside herself, that she meant no less than that. No less at all.

"When you've found out all you can about Beamsters," she said, "what will you do with what you've written?"

"I shan't be finished for ages," he said. "But as to what to do with it, I just don't know. You tell me to try to get it published, but I just can't believe anyone would want to read it."

"And I've told you before, they might."

"It would make a good memorial, I suppose. Mother would like that. '*The Beemasters*, my dear dead son's famous book, you know.'"

"Now you're being stupid again. I shan't stay."

He was contrite at once. "Sorry, Katy-Cat. When the time comes that I'm satisfied with the script, I'll send it off to a publisher if you like. They'll probably tell me quite politely that I'd better take up fair-isle knitting instead."

"Make it crochet," said Cathy. "It's prettier." He slung a cushion at her, but she fielded it neatly and went to look for the Scrabble board. As she found it, Mrs. Anderson came in. Cathy hoped Mark would be pleasant to her. She had mastered her anxiety so well when he had been riding this afternoon. It wasn't her fault that she was such a worrier, and she really had tried hard. She deserved something in return, Cathy felt.

"Hello, Mum," he said, as she sat down in her chair, looking gray and tired. "Have a game of Scrabble."

It was a needle game, with much recourse to the dictionary and considerable argument about the validity of some of Mark's words, as he did tend to invent if he could not find one to the purpose. It was a good evening, though, and Cathy was pleased to see Mark not so much at odds with his mother, whose tiredness seemed to have evaporated.

Cathy was late to bed, and weary with the events of the day, but even so she was determined to look through the articles on bees that Mr. Burton had sent for her. There was a good deal of heavy reading in them, so that once or twice she nearly fell asleep onto the opened page, and there were some quotations in Latin from early authors on the subject, which foxed her entirely, as she had not yet got beyond Caesar throwing his baggage over the river. There were some good reprints of illustrations from some of the old books though: she especially liked the crabbed woodcuts from William Lawson's *Country Housewife's Garden*, showing how bees were kept in Tudor times, when every farmer's wife kept bees for her own use, much as her mother kept backyard hens now. They wouldn't have had the Beemaster's skill and wisdom though, she was sure of that. She could see him in her mind, the Beemaster: different in every generation, yet somehow the same person, the same presence, with skills that were almost magical. But it was a gentle, healing magic, not like the fierce craft of the smith. She remembered the burnt-horn smell of the man who had come to put shoes on Moirag, the day after she had arrived, and the white heat of the metal where it lay in his portable forge, dulling to red in the air, and dying to gray as he plunged the shoes he had fashioned into a bucket of water to cool them. No wonder the smiths had been thought of as powerful men, and not only for their physique. The Beemaster's power was more subtle.

The more she read, the more she knew she wanted the bees to come back to Beamsters. The house felt the lack of them: she was convinced of that. She was pleased then when her mother said next day that she'd heard from the woman who worked for Mrs. Roberts that if they wanted any honey later in the year, Mr. Agar, who lived beyond Rook's Point, had hives in his garden and had honey to sell, and beeswax for polish if you liked to make your own. Cathy decided to visit Mr. Agar and ask his advice, and find out all he could tell her about the keeping of bees.

He turned out to be very small, very old, and delighted to find someone interested in his craft. He showed her around his colonies, and explained how they were kept and cared for: he told her how the bees arranged their flights and gathered the nectar, and how they performed their strange secret dances. It was not like a lesson or a lecture. It was like being admitted to a fellowship.

She showed him the articles she had been reading. "Though you don't want to take much notice of what these fellows say," he remarked. "They rarely wrote from their own experience. They copied what the Romans said about bees, for the most part."

She began to spend so many hours with Mr. Agar that Mark became disgruntled, and Cathy's conscience began to prickle because she had not made more effort where Fiona was concerned. She had tried. She had invited her

[97]

to Beamsters, for tea, and been taken on a couple of disastrous outings by Mrs. Harris, which had only made Fiona draw further away than ever. As for Moirag, Fiona would not go near her, almost as if she were afraid, though she did not show fear. It was more like distaste.

Mark's annoyance with Cathy did not last long when she told him all she had learned from Mr. Agar.

"Perhaps we'll get bees back here again after all," he teased her. "Now you're such an expert."

"That'll be the day. Do you want to ride this afternoon? Mrs. Johnson will be here."

"What about the frightful Fiona?" he asked.

"She might come. I don't know." Cathy felt defensive, prickly.

"I wish you didn't have to bother with that misery. Why do you waste your time on her?"

"I haven't wasted much recently. She can't help being as she is."

"One miserable wonky hand. She could help that all right. If she'd do her physio I'm sure she could get more movement in it. She just doesn't try."

Cathy dropped the subject, but all through the midday meal she was very quiet and thoughtful until she saw her mother looking hard at her.

"Mum, I think we've got it the wrong way around."

"Got what the wrong way around?"

"Fiona. I don't think she hates the idea of riding because she's damaged her hand. I think she doesn't want her hand to get better because she's scared silly to ride. I think her nerve went after that fall. If she's *able* to ride, you see, her mother will expect her to, but if her hand is useless, she's excused."

"That must have taken some working out," Jean Marshall said. "You might be right, though, Cath. Still, I don't see that it makes your job any easier."

"She won't touch Moirag. Won't come near her. Getting her to do that might be the first step."

"It's worth trying, dear."

Fiona did come that afternoon, and trailed about the yard while Cathy got Moirag ready. Mark was in his wheelchair by the stable door, watching.

"Fiona!" Cathy called out from the shadows of the stable. "Can you help me? This strap's stuck." There was a long pause. Then Mark bowled himself slowly over to where Fiona was standing. He had been a little more mobile these last few days. After a few moments Fiona came, with obvious reluctance, into the stable where Cathy was pretending to have difficulty with the girth.

"What's the matter?" Fiona asked in a voice as cold as pebbles.

"Something's wrong with this: it won't pull up properly."

"You've got the strap through the wrong part of the buckle."

"I can't see what you mean. Will you show me?"

"Anyone could do it."

"I can't," Cathy said, doggedly. Fiona sighed; a sigh that lucidly expressed her contempt for Cathy's stupidity. She took the girth strap with her good hand and adjusted it correctly. Cathy, peering over her shoulder as if to see how to do it next time, just happened to lean against her a little so that Fiona's hand just brushed the pony's side, and her knuckle rested for an instant on the warm, golden coat.

Later, when Mark was riding and they were away from the others, Cathy asked him how he had persuaded Fiona to come.

"Persuaded, my eye," he said. "I told her I thought it was her hand she's lost the use of, not her legs."

"Ouch."

"Don't waste your sympathy. It's time the Dismal Daughter stopped feeling sorry for herself. That's my prerogative."

He turned himself as far as he could in the saddle and called out to Fiona, "Hey. Want a ride?"

"Are you speaking to me?"

"Of course I'm speaking to you. The Queen of Sheba couldn't come, so we've got to put up with you instead. Have a ride. I'm sure you could do it better than me." Cathy could have kicked him. As she expected, Fiona turned and walked away without another word. Mark continued to enjoy his ride, but Cathy's heart had gone out of it. She felt heavy all over as she plodded about, leading Moirag. Then Jenny Barnes and Eileen Johnson came over to suggest that Mark might try trotting, very slowly, to see how it felt.

"I'll leave you to it," Cathy said. "I'd better go and find Fiona."

"Suit yourself," Mark said. "I shan't fall off just because you're not watching."

As she walked toward the house in search of Fiona, she heard his breathless laughter as he tried to adjust himself to the faster motion. "Damn Fiona," Cathy thought, her heart as heavy as her legs.

Ten

"Divide and rule," Cathy thought to herself. As far as she could she would separate Mark and Fiona; only see the one in the absence of the other. It would not be possible all the time, of course, but as she seemed landed with helping them both, and they reacted to each other so badly, they were best kept apart.

With the lengthening of the summer days there was time to ride between homework and bed. Eileen Johnson taught Cathy whenever she could spare the time, and Cathy, though she knew she would never be the best of riders, enjoyed the easy exercises, and the sense of harmony with Moirag. It made her realize, too, what effort Mark must put into it, with his weakened muscles and his lack of coordination. Courage and sheer enjoyment seemed to compensate for the lack of these things and his accomplishment as a rider amazed them all.

With Fiona, progress was slower. Cathy used every trick she could think of to get her near the pony, to handle her, to accept her presence. She could see how one half of Fiona struggled with the other. She wants to ride again really, Cathy felt now. She is afraid that being near Moirag will make her want it too much. And she is afraid of being afraid if she tries again. Cathy was determined to win in the end. It would be so much easier if she liked the girl, but it was like trying to befriend a shadow. What was needed, Cathy supposed, was some storybook situation where Fiona would be forced to mount Moirag and gallop through the night on some desperate errand, to fetch the doctor or the fire brigade, or to warn the neighborhood of some impending doom. However, as there were two fully operational telephones at hand, and no one was in any imminent danger from anything other than sunburn as the weather improved, that solution of the problem seemed very unlikely. She did, however, notice Fiona occasionally slipping like a shadow into Moirag's stable when the pony was standing indoors waiting to start her work, or escaping from the hot sun and the flies. Cathy had pretended she had not noticed these visits of Fiona's, but she did wish she could see through the wall to discover what was happening in the stable.

Once, when Cathy woke very early, at first light, disturbed by some unknown unease, she was unable to see Moirag in the field, when she went to her window and looked out. She was not disturbed by this for there were corners of the field where a pony could stand hidden, and the fences were sound and the gate secure. However, when she went down after breakfast to catch the pony for her father, it seemed to her that Moirag was warmer than usual, and there was a faint patch of sweat where the saddle would rest. *Mark* could not ride the pony without help. The first time she noticed, Cathy laughed at herself for playing Sherlock Holmes, but a few days later it happened again, so she set her alarm for daybreak the next morning. She got out of her warm bed to no purpose though, for she neither heard nor saw anything out of the ordinary.

By mid-May Mark was riding very much under his own control, steering Moirag with the special reins Eileen Johnson had brought him, which his often awkward and clumsy hands could cope with more easily than the usual kind. Cathy watched him, mobile, independent and radiating cheerfulness, riding about in the shade of the trees at the field edge, encouraged by Jenny Barnes. She wished that Fiona were doing as well. It worried Cathy, that apart from being perhaps a little less shadowlike, Fiona seemed much as she had always been. Mrs. Harris made no comment, but Cathy felt sure she must be bitterly disappointed. It wasn't for the want of trying, Cathy argued with her troubled conscience, but Mark's dislike of the girl was no help at all.

"Try walking over those poles now, Mark," Jenny Barnes was saying. "Your balance is quite good enough. Time for a bit more progress."

"Watch it Harvey Smith." Mark grinned. "Competition's on its way."

That day was the last of the fine weather for a while. In the evening gray banks of cloud loomed over the treetops and huge, wet drops spattered the ground as, in the distance, thunder began to mutter and grumble to itself.

From the comforting thickness of the walls of the old house, Cathy waited for the storm. Moirag, out in the field, lifted her head and sniffed into the wind, then turned as the rain began to slant down and hunched herself into it, solid as a boulder, not worried at all by the fizzle and crack of lightning and the angry noises from the sky. Then the rain hurled itself so hard at the windowpanes that everything outside was hidden.

Her father came to ask her if she minded the storm, and she said she was OK, but what about Moirag?

"She'll be happier out there, I think. In a stable the noises might seem worse. Anyway, when I looked, she was standing quite quietly, and she's well away from the trees. I only hope the cattle will be as sensible."

Having broken so dramatically, the weather became set in its ways and blew up rainy and cold for a week, making riding impossible and Mark bad tempered. A ride in the rain may be exhilarating if you travel fast and keep the blood moving, but to go slowly is to be soaked through and uncomfortable in no time, with the searching wetness finding its way cold to the skin.

Deprived of his exercise, Mark became increasingly gloomy, so Mrs. Anderson took him shopping, hoping to cheer him up. He needed some clothes and she promised to take him to the bookshop afterward so that he could browse around. Burfords' was the best kind of bookshop. There you could spend hours thumbing through books, and even reading them from cover to cover if you wanted to, without being disturbed or pressed into buying. Indeed, there were two elderly gentlemen who appeared to spend all their time there, tucked into a corner of the Classics section, from the moment the shop opened until the closing bell. Possibly they did not go home even then, but read by moonlight and were dusted off with the books next day.

Cathy was tempted to join the outing, but she had some schoolwork to get through, and there was still a good deal of decorating to be done at Beamsters as well, so she waved the car off down the road, and then went back indoors to her various jobs. In fact she became so busy that the day just vanished, and it was midafternoon before she and Mrs. Marshall even realized it was long past time for a meal.

"That was a good day's work, Mum," Cathy said. "One painted wall, three algebra exercises, one roomful of stained floorboards, and an essay on Keats and Shelley."

"Do you think I'll get my O-levels in Painting and Decorating?" Mrs. Marshall laughed.

"You've decorated yourself more than anything, Mum," Cathy said. "You've got white paint in your hair and on your nose and floor stain on your hands."

"You aren't all that clean yourself, miss! What's more, you've got ink and felt pen to add to your color scheme. We'd better both go and get cleaned up and then have a sandwich."

When she had removed the traces of her day's occupation, Cathy decided she'd go over to the bungalow. The car had come back, and she wanted to find out if Mark had bought anything interesting. The rain had stopped for the first time that day, and Cathy felt bouncy and cheerful, and full of that pleasurable feeling you get when you've done all you set out to do. In fact she was in such a state of "God's in his heaven, all's right with the world" as she opened the bungalow door and headed for the kitchen, that it was a shock to realize that someone was sobbing bitterly. It was Mrs. Anderson. She was sitting at the kitchen table, facing away from Cathy, with her head in her hands and her shoulders shaking. She looked so lonely and so miserable, but Cathy was not sure whether she would want anyone with her. Her own parents were so cheerful and happy together that she had had very little experience of adults crying, but

[105]

she hovered in the doorway, making her presence known, to give Mrs. Anderson a chance to ask her to go away, if that was what she wanted.

After a while, making a great effort to control her weeping, Mark's mother blew her nose hard, and spoke to Cathy, though she would not look at her.

"I'm sorry, my dear," she said. "Try not to take any notice of me. It's been a bad day. If you've come to see Mark you won't find him any better company than me, I'm afraid. Something upset him terribly this morning."

She paused, and Cathy waited, unable to find anything to say, feeling very uncomfortable.

Mrs. Anderson turned her head at last; her face under control now.

"Cathy, I'll tell you, though you may think it a trivial thing to make the two of us so miserable. It was such a shame though, and so unnecessary. If only people would think! Mark and I were waiting outside the chemist's for Miss Barnes—she'd gone to collect a prescription for someone—when some silly, well-meaning woman came up and started to talk to me, saying how sorry she was to see my little boy was in a wheelchair. Poor old Mark, I know he looks younger than he is, but 'little boy,' I ask you. Then she went on and on talking to me, talking *at* me really, about Mark, right across him, as if he could not understand a word she said. It was horrible, but I just could not get out the words to stop her, and I could see Mark going whiter and whiter, until at last he really screamed at her, 'I'm a cripple, Madam, not a lunatic. If anyone around here needs certifying, it's you!' Then the woman got angry, of course, and by the time Miss Barnes came out of the shop we were all pretty hysterical."

"Oh, Mrs. Anderson, I am so sorry. What a rotten thing to happen."

"Thank you, Cathy dear. You've known us long enough to have realized that Mark and I don't live easily together at the best of times, and when this sort of thing happens it's well-nigh impossible for me to get near him. It's my own fault, I know. I should treat him just as I'd treat anyone else who is rude and ill-mannered, but he feels special to me. He *is* special to me. It's been a long, hard fight."

"Would it help if I went and sat with him for a while?" Cathy asked. She didn't want to. She felt angry for him, but she did not want to face him.

"You can try, my dear. Good luck."

"Thanks," said Cathy.

When she went into the room where Mark sat, she knew she would need all the good luck she could get. There would be no snapping him out of this with a joke or a sharp remark. She sat down by the window and began to read a book she found there; it was a book of seventeenth-century sermons; not really to her taste at the best of times, but she forced herself to follow the print and to take in each word as it presented itself. More often than not, though, her eye would rebel, and retrace the same sentence over and over again, so that phrases, sensible in their context, danced and swam in her mind, nonsensical and meaningless.

At last, though, Mark, who had sat completely still for a long time, began to relax and move, and the wheelchair came across toward Cathy. He spoke to her, abruptly.

"Do you want some tea?"

"Yes, please."

[107]

He looked at her long and hard.

"Thank you for not being all jolly," he said, and trundled off into the kitchen. For a while Cathy could hear nothing of what was going on, but eventually the cups and plates began their cheerful chatter, and there was the sound of conversation between Mark and his mother, quite sane and happy, with no note of tension or dissension about it.

Mark and Cathy had a good evening together, with the rain once more falling outside, and books spread out on the table before them. Mrs. Anderson left them to it, and went to bed early with her radio for company. She had found the day long enough.

They began once again to talk about the bees, the once honored residents of Beamsters, who now no longer seemed to want to live there; and Mark thought he had found a clue to their disappearance from the garden. Apparently they had flourished as always until well after the Restoration, even though there had been a slump in beekeeping then, with fewer church candles needed, and mead out of favor with the coming in of wine from abroad. Even so, the hives at Beamsters had not suffered, and indeed were praised by John Keys, the writer of *The Practical Beemaster,* when he came to visit Geoffrey Manders, who was Master of the property in those days. Geoffrey was a good, conscientious man, and so was his son, Jacob, but Jacob was full of the new curiosity that was beginning to develop—a thing they called "science," which caused people to want to know the how and the wherefore of the working of things; even of things as ordinary and everyday as the bee.

Jacob drove his father to distraction, with watching the bees for hours, and drawing them.

"He even used to cut up dead bees to see how they

were made inside," Mark said, "and he wrote books and books of notes and observations. Well, of course, old Geoffrey carried all his knowledge and experience in his head and felt that all this study was a waste of time. He was an old man and liked the old ways, and every time Jacob came up with some new theory there would be the devil's own argument about it. Geoffrey wanted to go on managing the bees as he had always done, killing off the old hives at honey-taking, and getting his new stock from swarms. He could see no use for the old colonies, and thought they would only be a nuisance if he didn't destroy them. But Jacob, from all his watching and studying, thought it was needless cruelty, and felt sure it would be possible to design hives with movable frames, so that honey could be taken out without having to kill off the bees. Then, if the bees could be fed through the winter, they'd survive and work again the following season, and any new stock from swarms would be a bonus instead of a replacement."

"Surely old Geoffrey must have seen it was the better way?" Cathy said.

"Old men don't like change," Mark replied. "I expect when they stopped killing off all the cows each winter and started bringing them into the yards and feeding them on roots and good hay, the old chaps of the day probably muttered and grumbled and thought the sky would fall in!"

"I suppose you're right. What happened in the end though, between Geoffrey and Jacob?"

"I'm afraid their arguments must have flared into a full-scale quarrel, because Mr. Burton has a copy of a letter that Jacob wrote to the old man from London, saying he was not coming back to Beamsters. Apparently he'd taken up with a character called Thomas

[109]

Wildman, who used to lecture about bees, and did a sort of circus act with them. He'd let them crawl all over him, and then they'd mass around his chin like a beard. Perhaps he was a charlatan, I don't know, but he seems to have known his stuff where bees were concerned, and Jacob was fascinated.

"There's no other record of Jacob after that, but poor old Geoffrey was so worried, or angry, or both, that he went out one day and burned all the bees in their hives, and every book and piece of equipment his son had left behind. He came within an ace of burning the house too, but the Constable fetched him away, and he died in Bedlam at the end of the year."

"Poor old man," Cathy said. "Fancy being taken from a place like this, to die in a madhouse."

"Poor Beamsters too," Mark added. "It stood empty a good many years after that, and the garden ran riot and part of the roof fell in. Then it was bought for a pound or so and put to rights again, but there was no luck to be had with keeping bees here. It was as if the ghosts of all the old Beemasters had risen up to warn them off."

Eleven

Once or twice, during that rainy time, the saddle and bridle that Mark was unable to use had seemed to Cathy suspiciously damp.

She mentioned this to Mark on the first day he was able to ride.

"You don't think it could possibly be the DD, do you?"

She seemed the only likely person; and yet the least likely person. Admittedly Cathy had noticed her slip into Moirag's stable, thinking herself unseen, on several occasions, yet she still seemed, in herself, as nervous and withdrawn as ever.

Mark mentioned the subject again that evening as he and Cathy sat listening to records in the sitting room at Lawn End. Cathy's parents had been asked away for the night, and Mrs. Anderson had invited her to sleep at the bungalow. Mark did more than mention Fiona and her mother. His character assassination of both of them was devastating, clever and extremely funny. So much so that by the end of it both he and Cathy were almost paralyzed with laughter. He took off on the county accents of Mrs. Harris and the flat hesitations of Fiona's voice until the tears ran down Cathy's face. Mrs. Anderson was in the room, but she did not seem to be very much amused. Still she did not know the Horsey Horror and the Dismal Daughter all that well.

There was only just enough light to see by when Mark woke Cathy in the morning.

"Come quick!" he said. "You'll never believe what I've just been watching."

Cathy rolled out of bed, startled and sleepy, and stumbled after him to where his wide window overlooked the garden and, beyond it, the Beamsters field.

Fiona was riding Moirag. She was riding her not as Mark and Cathy rode: Mark, making a brave try, but limited by his disease; Cathy, still very new to the skill, and unsure of her balance. This was riding like a dance, like a dream, in the gray mist that rose from the dew-soaked grass and floated in ragged drifts over the field. Moirag, their stolid, slow and trusted conveyor of feed sacks and less than competent riders, was covering the ground in an alert and cadenced canter, a beautiful, harmonious rhythm of which Fiona was a part, as she sat secure and still at the center from which all this movement sprang.

Mark and Cathy sat watching, amazed and entranced.

"She must have been practicing, all this time," Cathy said.

Mark let out a long breath. "She's good," he said.

"Yes, isn't she?" Janet Anderson stood behind them. They had not heard her enter the room. "She comes almost every morning. I don't sleep much once it begins to be light, and I've watched her since the first time. White as a sheet she was then and shaking with fright, leading Moirag as if she was a bomb that might go off

[112]

at any minute. It took her half an hour the first morning just to pluck up the courage to get on."

"Why didn't you tell us?" Mark protested.

"It was obviously meant to be a secret," his mother said. "It wasn't my business to tell. I thought she'd let you know when she was ready. I hadn't realized you thought her such a joke. She has worked so hard, and every time she has come she has found it that little bit easier. She spends about an hour out there, and then she walks back home again. That must be a couple of miles at least. Today, for the first time, I've noticed she had the reins in two hands. She must be getting a little use back in the left one.

"Now perhaps you see why I didn't think your performance last night was amusing, Mark. *You* hate to be labeled, don't you? 'He's a cripple. Pity him!'?"

She was angry now. Cathy saw Mark wince, but his mother went on. "Once you've labeled people you don't have to think any further, do you? You know exactly how to treat them. 'He's a gypsy: he must be a thief. She's a witch: burn her. He's a criminal: chuck him in jail. She's horsey: laugh at her.' Easy isn't it? Well, people are more than their labels, Mark. Mrs. Harris may bray like a trumpet and look like Horse and Hound, but she's a mum worried sick about her daughter, just as I, for my sins, worry myself sick about you. As for Fiona, she was crippled every bit as much as you"—Mrs. Anderson whipped the word out at him like a lash, and it stung him—"and like you she's had the courage to fight it. You've seen what she can do, and I think she deserves your friendship, not your ridicule."

His mother turned away and left the room, and Mark sat with his mouth open as if his jaw had become unhinged, and stared after her. At last, after a long silence, he shook himself, and said, "Wow! What's bitten her?"

"We were rather horrible last night," Cathy suggested.

"Don't be a prig," Mark snapped, but Cathy could see he was staggered by his mother's outburst.

"She hasn't spoken to me like that for years," he said.

Perhaps she should have, Cathy thought to herself. They were being pretty nasty, there's no use denying. Now, somehow, they must find a way of making friends with Fiona and persuading her to allow the world to know that she had been riding again. Goodness only knew. If they got it wrong they could destroy everything for her, including the early-morning sessions with Moirag that she still, up to this moment, thought were her secret.

Cathy wished that life did not develop quite so many complications, one after another.

When she had breakfasted with the Andersons—both very quiet, very particularly polite to each other—she went across to Beamsters to feed the hens and to fetch her bicycle ready for school. She bowled along the road to Bucklehurst, the wheels making a pleasant noise on the tarmac, the air fresh in her face. She was pleased with the morning, pleased with the essay that was her offering to the English teacher, not so pleased with herself for her efforts with Fiona. She saw again in her mind the girl on the golden horse in the early light. She must look for the substance under the shadow.

It was Mark who solved it, though. Mark who persuaded Cathy to get Moirag ready for a ride that evening, though there was no one there to help but Cathy herself, and Fiona, who had been sent over that day as a rather reluctant guest for tea. Mr. and Mrs. Marshall were not due back for another hour. Janet Anderson was visiting a friend; no one else was about.

Getting Mark onto the pony was no problem now. Moirag stood like a rock while he heaved and clambered into the saddle, supported by Cathy, and then he rode off so briskly that Cathy could scarcely keep up. He rode about much as usual for a few minutes, then, suddenly, he turned Moirag's head and urged her into a trot toward where Fiona was standing. It was a smarter pace than he had ever dared before. He seemed to be no longer in control. His hands were high and his balance was going.

"Help me, please, Fiona!" If it was acting, it was consummate acting. She reacted swiftly. She ran toward him and seized the bridle, catching him as he almost fell. Indeed, he was so far out of the saddle that when Cathy caught up, the safest thing seemed to be to slither him to the ground, where he sat looking like a bird that had forgotten how to fly, drooping, wings outspread and head low.

"I'm a bit shaky," he said at last. "Cathy, could you bring my chair? Fiona can ride Moirag back."

She began to protest, but he grinned, devilish, but kindly. "The game's up you know. We saw you. You're a treat to watch. I wish you'd show us again."

The faintest tinge of pink brightened Fiona's colorless face for a moment. It could have been embarrassment. Cathy hoped it was pleasure. Whatever it was, it made a reality out of Fiona. She paused only a moment to stare at Mark, then she swung up onto Moirag's back and rode away from them in a wide circle around the field. She came back to them in a rush of thudding hoofs, and her back was straight and her eyes were bright and she was beginning to think about smiling.

"Smashing," said Mark, his face alight, admiring her skill.

"OK?" Cathy asked her, wanting assurance more for herself than for Fiona.

"OK," Fiona said.

"Right, then I'll go and fetch the chair for this fallen knight before he gets a cold in his backside." She glowered at him. "Which is just where he deserves to get one."

Twelve

Inside the old house the air was cool and pleasant. Clean white walls shone pale against the dark timbers, and in the dogleg corners of the passageway and the stairs, Jean Marshall had set great bunches of summer flowers in the copper pots that had come with the house when Great-uncle John bought it. Flower arranging was no delicate art as far as she was concerned. She would thrust a great sheaf of blooms into the vase and say, "Go on, then, sit up and look beautiful." And they did.

Cathy paced about the house, pleased that it looked so cared-for now, pleased to feel part of it: pleased too that Mark had told her that morning that he had sent off his typescript to a publisher.

"It's bound to come back," he had told her.

"There are plenty of publishers. You'll have to keep on trying," she had replied.

Then he had laughed and said, "Those old Egyptians should have had you around. They could have had twice the pyramids in half the time."

She was alone in the house, and its rooms were quiet.

She spoke softly to all that was past in it: all the history in its fabric: all the people who had loved it and lived in it as she did now. Afterward she had no memory of what words she had used, but it had been a conversation with a friend; easy and happy.

Then she went out into the bright dazzle of the June garden, into the first real heat-wave day of the year. Her parents were lying in garden chairs under the shade of a lime tree. It was a day to make anyone feel sleepy and lazy.

She went and joined them, and saw that in the field, Moirag and the cattle were also standing in the deep shade of the trees away from the pestering flies. It was too hot to ride, too hot even to think for long.

"I wish I could swim," Cathy said, but they none of them felt like the drive to the coast, in a hot car in a line of others with the same thing in mind.

"The swimming pools will be crowded too," said Mrs. Marshall.

"That'll be the next thing, Joe. Dig us a swimming pool!"

"Right-oh," Joe Marshall said, equably. "And there's room for a tennis court up there, and a croquet lawn as well if you like, and what about a polo ground? The field's about the right size."

Jean Marshall threw a twig from the lime tree at him.

"Don't be daft," she said. "It would be nice, though, wouldn't it: a cool splash when the weather's hot like this. We could get young Mark in the water."

"He'd like that," Cathy said.

"Twice a summer, if you're lucky, we get it as hot as this. All that work, just for two swims a year. You must be joking." Joe Marshall sat up in his chair and stretched himself in a broad yawn. "Where is that boy, anyway?"

"Gone to his therapy group," Cathy said. "I said he could ride this evening if it's cooler."

"He really enjoys it, doesn't he?" said her mother.

"It's a treat to see him on that pony. It's cheered him up no end. He's beginning to be nicer to his mum, too. None too soon."

"I've got quite fond of that boy," Joe Marshall remarked.

"Think of him as the son you never had, do you?" Cathy teased.

"Probably," he retorted. "Who'd live by choice in a house full of women?"

His own women, incensed by this remark, threatened to collapse his chair with him in it, but suddenly, in mid action, Cathy stood still. "Listen a minute," she said.

Among the summer noises of the garden was one that had seized her attention: one that she could not at first interpret. Then she saw what it was.

"Dad! Mum!" she said, urgently. "Look over there! We've got a swarm of bees in the garden!"

Joe Marshall stopped his fooling and looked where she was pointing. On one of the branches of the acacia tree nearest the house hung a pear-shaped mass of bees, piercing the afternoon with their noise. They could only just have arrived, for they were still jostling with each other for position, and one or two, still in the air, were looking for a clinging place.

"Well, I never," said Joe Marshall. "Where did they come from?"

"I'll phone Mr. Agar, shall I?" Cathy suggested. Mr. Agar was delighted when he heard the bees were in the Marshall's garden. They were, indeed, his bees, he said,

[119]

and they had gathered once in his own garden, but a dog had disturbed them and they had taken flight again. He said he would come over and bring a skep. Then he seemed to think again, for he coughed and muttered to himself in a way that Cathy had discovered was a habit with him when there was something on his mind.

"It seems to me," he said, after a while, "that as they have seen fit to come to the Beemaster's garden, they might care to stay there. What would you think of that? I could help you; advise you if you need it, if you care to look after them."

Cathy told him what she thought of that. She could not say that it was just what the old house had been waiting for: only that she would like to have the chance to keep the bees at Beamsters.

"Fine," he said. "I'll bring a hive. We'll see if they'll settle."

"He's bringing a hive," she told her parents. "He thinks they might want to stay here."

"Well then," said Joe Marshall—to whom Cathy had retold a great deal of the history of the bees that Mark had set down—"you'd best go and invite them."

She walked across the grass to where the swarm hung from the branch of the acacia tree, and stood looking up at the pear-shaped bundle of brown furry shapes, their quivering wings blurred with motion as they stirred and settled. Quietly she spoke to them, confident and unafraid.

"You have come to the Beemaster's house," she told them. "If you will stay here, Mark and I will care for you. Stay with us, please."

Gradually, at the sound of her words, their deep, excited, communal voice dropped to a quiet murmur, and as Cathy watched, they stilled their wings until there was scarcely a movement to be seen. There was no more noise than the sound of summer in its course.

The bees were home.